VETERAN SEWING MACHINES

VETERAN
SEWING MACHINES

A Collector's Guide

BRIAN JEWELL

South Brunswick and New York:
A. S. BARNES and COMPANY

© 1975 by BRIAN JEWELL

Library of Congress Catalog Card Number: 74-30539

First American Edition Published 1975
A. S. Barnes and Company, Inc.,
Cranbury, New Jersey 08512

ISBN 0-498-01714-1
Printed in Great Britain

CONTENTS

LIST OF ILLUSTRATIONS

7

List of Illustrations

8

PREFACE

This book has two aims: to act as a guide for collectors of sewing machines and to give a history of the invention and development of these machines. We believe it to be the first guide of its kind. Historically, the known facts that have emerged during some five years of research into the industrial history of nineteenth-century Britain, America and European countries are all documented.

Any definition of the term veteran, when applied to sewing machines, must be arbitrary. Collectors have their own ideas: some consider 1900 as a terminal date, while others prefer to extend their terms of reference to 1914, 1925 and even 1950. It would, I am sure, be a disservice to collectors to introduce complex classifications such as those used in connection with historic motor vehicles —veteran, vintage, Edwardian, post-vintage, classic and so on. So, for the purpose of this book, the term veteran has been used to cover sewing machines built up to 1925. By that year almost all the important ingredients for the modern sewing machine were being used and the industry had settled down to a firmly based pattern.

In preparing this book I owe a considerable debt of gratitude to the works of Mrs Grace Rogers Cooper, Curator of Textiles, The Smithsonian Institution, Washington, DC, and one of her predecessors, Dr Frederick L. Lenton. Without such a foundation the compilation of material would have been a formidable task.

Preface

I am aware that there is still a great amount of ground to be covered, both in the figurative and literal senses. Much of this kind of research can only be carried out in the neighbourhood of the industrially productive centres in the countries concerned.

It can be argued that a complete background to the sewing machine will never be compiled, so much valuable reference material having been lost. I am always anxious to hear from people who may be in possession of information on known marques of sewing machines, as well as, of course, hitherto unrecorded makes.

This book will achieve its purpose if more people are encouraged to interest themselves in this wondrous example of Victorian invention, and if it helps confirmed enthusiasts to identify, or presents additional information about, the machines in their collection.

Brian Jewell,
Tunbridge Wells,
1974

INTRODUCTION

It was in May 1971 that Lt-Col Eric Barrass, Secretary of the Rolls-Royce Owners' Club and organiser of the Pageant of Motoring, held annually at Penshurst Place in Kent, asked the author if he had any ideas for a new display theme at the pageant. For several years prior to this, the Broadwater Collection of Transport Models—commemorating the world's first horseless carriage exhibition at Tunbridge Wells in 1895—had been displayed at the pageant. A number of early sewing machines and typewriters had been introduced into the collection over the previous months, and it was agreed that a Rally of Veteran Sewing Machines would be staged.

At the time, apart from some exchanges of correspondence with the Smithsonian Institution, Washington, and the Science Museum, London, no contact had been made with other sewing machine collectors and museums. Consequently, it was with some trepidation that the Broadwater Collection machines, augmented by a Jenny Lind, on loan from Singer's Guildford, Surrey, depot, and some exhibits from a local museum and sewing machine shop, were set up on display.

The machines had been mentioned on the pageant's press release and such an unusual collection had been commented on in some of the national press. The BBC Radio programme, 'Today', carried a two-minute interview and a recording of some of the machines in operation. 'Sewing machines, very light on fuel, but not so good up hill'—after all the Penshurst gathering is a motoring event—was the commentator's joking remark.

It might have been a joke to some but, within an hour of the opening, it became clear that the sewing machines were being taken very seriously indeed by a large number of people. Those who had heard mention of Singer's Jenny Lind on the radio, and who normally did not care for veteran car events, were arriving from far and wide. Sewing machine enthusiasts were bringing along their Wheeler & Wilsons, Howes and Weirs. The first rally of veteran sewing machines was in progress.

By the end of the day it had been decided that there was a need for a Register to record the locations and owners of historic machines—not restricted solely to sewing machines—and for a newsletter (later to become *Bygone & Veteran* magazine) in which enthusiasts could exchange information. Within a few months collectors, including a number in the USA, Australia, Holland and Italy, were submitting details of machines in their possession. Each day brought its surprises, for example a parfilage or 'drizzling' winder—since acquired by the Broadwater Collection—made c1800, for the reclaiming of gold and silver thread from old uniforms.

Contacts have now been made with correspondents in many countries and it is apparent that there are many collections of veteran machinery already in existence, whilst the band of collectors increases almost daily. There is, however, a lack of detailed literature on the subject, and it is hoped that this volume will go some way towards filling that gap.

PART 1

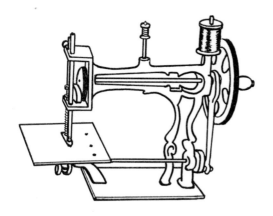

1

WHY SEWING MACHINES?

Today's junk is tomorrow's antique. Over the past few years it has become increasingly difficult to find *pure* antiques—furniture, silver, porcelain, paintings, and the like, over one hundred years of age—in good condition and at reasonable prices. Most of the more desirable items have already found homes with either collectors or investors. It is not really surprising therefore that many collectors are now looking to bygones—those items from a previous age that used to be called curiosities—and veteran machinery.

As the hard commercial world has its tentacles delving into the crannies of most collecting fields, it would be convenient to answer the question posed by the title of this chapter simply by observing that the value of veteran sewing machines is increasing at a greater rate than the cost of living. That would be misleading however. True, a c1896 Willcox & Gibbs machine, of similar date and condition to one picked up by the author at an auction sale for £2 two years before, was seen in a Sussex antique shop in the summer of 1973 priced at £18, but this is not a true indication of the market. A rarer machine, an early Weir, was sold in 1973 for £8, about what one would expect to pay or receive for a collectable model at that time. Exceptional and genuinely rare items will, of course, command higher prices, but if profit is to be the sole motive for collecting, there are richer pickings elsewhere. Some die-cast-model cars, for instance, can treble their list price in five or six years, but a hundred-year-old sewing machine can still be bought for considerably less than was paid for it when new.

The real reason why people collect veteran sewing machines, or other forms of mechanical antiques or bygones, for that matter, is that they *are* mechanical, reflecting the mechanics' inventive skill, the iron founder's craft and the stylists' art. It is very likely that a veteran sewing machine will perform the task for which it was built just as well today as it did a century ago, if not at once, then after slight curative treatment with an oil-can and screwdriver. One never ceases to be amazed at the reliability of a machine built in the early years of production of what was an innovation.

The sewing machine has a very special place among those items we call bygone or veteran. It was a surprising invention, for people of the first half of the nineteenth century were not exactly crying out 'we must have sewing machines': in fact, as will be shown later, the early inventors suffered from intense hostility. It was a most difficult machine to evolve. The remarkable fact is that it was invented when it was, at a time when the able mechanics who created it could have put their efforts into ideas that would have been more certain of bringing financial reward—and quicker.

From feeble attempts to copy the action of a sewing hand, to the conception of the chain- and lock-stitches, is a remarkable achievement. Just imagine, you wish to design a machine that will stitch two pieces of cloth together and the starting point is observation of a woman sitting in a poorly lit room with a needle between her fingers and with a single thread through an eye! Some inventors attempted to copy the motion of the human hand, substituting pincers for fingers. But the formula for a successful sewing machine was not to be found in this direction. The running-stitch and the back-stitch—the common stitches made by hand—were bylanes off the highway of mechanical sewing. The chain-stitch and the lock-stitch had to be devised before successful machines could be built to form them.

Apart from the clock, the sewing machine was the first industrially produced domestic mechanism. The ladies of the early 1850s were able to buy an entirely practical and dependable

Page 17 (*above*) Newton Wilson's
1874 chain-stitch machine
constructed from the original
specification of Saint's 1790 patent;
(*right*) replica of the first practical
chain-stitch machine invented by
Thimonnier in 1830

Page 18 (above) An early Grover & Baker cabinet model from 1856;
(below) Elias Howe's prepatent model of 1845

machine that would speed their sewing, but had to wait until 1876 before being able to purchase a mechanical carpet sweeper. A product of American industry at the time of the great Western adventure, many commercially produced sewing machines were trundled across the plains in covered waggons to be set up as an integral part of the settlers' homes. Machines were passed from mother to daughter and more than a few have come down to great-granddaughters.

Nineteenth-century sewing machines have lasted a good deal longer than examples of the then new-fangled horseless carriage. Perhaps this is one reason why the cult of the veteran car is well established and has been respectable for many years, carrying with it a certain prestige and the sweet smell of affluence—although by no means all veteran car owners are wealthy—whereas the enthusiasm for veteran sewing machines is a comparatively new interest. There are, however, a small number of owners, whose names appear on the Veteran Machine Register (see page 12), and who have been engaged in collecting sewing machines for more than twenty-five years.

Yet it is impossible to avoid comparison between cars and sewing machines. Both were the pride and joy of their original owners. Both have a diversity of designers', engineers' and artists' treatment. Both have individual personalities: the big, Teutonic Frister & Rossmanns of the 1900s have a similar aura to the Mercedes cars of the period. The Willcox & Gibbs can be compared with the 'curved-dash' Oldsmobile.

Singers, it may be said, are the Fords of the sewing machine world—but not in period. Isaac Merritt Singer brought mass-production methods to industry before Henry Ford was born. Ford took motoring to the masses. Singer and his partner, Clark, took mechanical sewing to even larger numbers of users, the salesmen carrying machines to remote corners of the world. As late as 1970, in Leningrad, USSR, there stood a battered and aged pre-revolution Singer sign on the roof of a building—the old depot—surviving war and the elements for over sixty years. One wonders why this symbol of Western capitalism had not been dismantled years before.

Venerable treadle New Family Singers are still in use in African villages and in Eastern bazaars.

As Model T Fords were put to every conceivable use, from powering saw benches to acting as railway locomotives, so the treadle Singer can claim the same sort of versatility, being used for marking out cardboard templates, for making rivet holes in thin metal sheets for model makers and for generating power for short-wave radios. There was at least one case in Holland, during World War II, of a cycle dynamo being bolted to a Singer to provide emergency lighting.

To the collector, veteran sewing machines have three considerable advantages over veteran motor vehicles: they take up a fraction of the space, maintenance is a good deal easier and, of supreme importance to many people, they are far cheaper. Of course there are shortcomings; there is no romance of the road about a sewing machine and no sporting connections! But an historic sewing machine can have as many outings in the course of a year as a veteran car, to be exhibited in special displays at motoring pageants and steam engine groups, or to take part in charity fund raising. The collector is never short of invitations to bring his machines to various events.

An important attraction in any new collecting interest is the research potential and, in the case of sewing machines, everyone can add to the knowledge bank. Not long ago it would have been surprising to see a magazine article devoted to bygone machinery—typewriters, mechanical toys, talking machines, domestic and kitchen equipment as well as sewing machines—especially in the art and antique press, but this is no longer exceptional. Now there is even a specialised publication, *Bygone & Veteran* (see page 12) for the owners of these very machines, which prides itself on being a vehicle for industrial history research.

And there is still much to discover, especially in the case of British and European machines. One puzzling character was a German inventor, S. A. Rosenthal, who patented a pocket sewing machine in 1885. This was a clamp-on-the-table type of device intended, it is said, for seamstresses who visited clients' homes where no sewing machines were available. It weighed about 1lb and measured only 8in by 2¾in by 1½in. The compact lock-stitch machine looked like a toy but incorporated every feature of a larger machine.

The machine was built by the Moldacot Pocket Sewing Machine Company, London, in 1886–7. The example on display in London's Science Museum carries the serial number 106,929 and another, in the author's collection, is numbered 107,332. Both these machines carry an anchor as a trademark. Another Moldacot among the Broadwater machines, serial number 6,385, is marked 'Patent London. Made in Germany', and carries a crown as a trademark. The latter machine is different from the first two in details, particularly in the design of the hand winder.

Who was Rosenthal and what other inventions should be accredited to him? Was the machine produced simultaneously in England and Germany? Why was the design patented in London?

Another toy machine was also built in Germany, in Nuremburg, and called The Princess (see Fig 1). This was cast in the shape of a woman sitting at her sewing. A surviving example changed hands in November 1973 for £100. Who, one wonders, were the manufacturers? How many machines like this were made and what was the period of production?

Questions like these can, and will be answered in time, as there continues to be an exchange of information amongst collectors. In the meantime, enthusiasts gain satisfaction from other aspects of research. The testimonials from early sewing machine users, for example, make interesting reading. In their c1873 publicity material, S. Smith & Company of Soho Bazaar, London, print a number of recommendations, including one, of which they were obviously proud, from the Nawab Nazim of Bengal. More interesting for the historian was one from a Mr J. Grove of New Zealand, written on 28 March 1870:

'The Agenoria machine, I am glad to say, is in excellent order, and we are getting quite masters of it. Mrs Grove sewed with it the first time of trying and she made a pair of trousers for me with it out of one of the two pieces of cloth a few days only after we had unpacked it. She has made sheets out of shirting calico, hemmed towels, made me a flannel shirt, some drawers for diggers, and done no end of sewing besides. Myself and wife consider the Franklin Company Machine an article that every family should have and be grateful for.'

Fig 1   The Nuremburg-built Princess toy sewing machine

2

EARLY DAYS: FROM SAINT TO SINGER

It is a sad fact that, unless by a miracle, a collector has no chance of procuring any of the machines referred to in the early part of this chapter. However, it is important that attention be paid to the early days of invention, if only to understand and compare later days of success and exploitation.

Although credit for the development of the sewing machine must rightly go to the Americans, there can be no doubt that its conception occurred in Europe and, to no mean extent, in England. Successful mechanical sewing has one indispensable ingredient— a needle, with both the point and the eye at the same end. Such a needle was invented in 1755 by a German mechanic living and working in London, one Charles F. Weisenthal, who was granted British patent no 701 in that year. True the needle had points at both ends as it was intended for use in embroidery and had this arrangement to avoid the necessity of turning the needle to complete a stitch but, without knowing it, Weisenthal had laid the foundation for the sewing machine.

Thirty-five years later, in 1790, again in London, Thomas Saint, a cabinet maker near Smithfield Market, received patent no 1764, covering a machine for stitching leather. Saint's sewing machine specification and drawings were accompanied by those of two other inventions, a woolcombing apparatus and a braid-making machine. Because of this variety of items, Saint's patent lay undiscovered for years on the Patent Office shelves. It was found by Newton Wilson, himself a manufacturer of sewing machines, who wrote in the *Journal of Domestic Appliances and Sewing Machine Gazette*, 2 November 1891:

'I think it was about the year 1874,[1] that examining some patents for boots and shoes in the library of the Patent Office, I came across one of ancient date, going back in fact to the last century. This was nominally for inventions of cements . . . but right in the heart of the specification was a single sheet of drawings . . . and . . . occupying the central position in the sheet, the drawing of a sewing machine . . .

'I gazed at that sheet with infinite interest. Here surely was the first idea of a sewing machine! A compound of wood and metal! The framework all wood, the movements all metal. The material to be sewn held by two clamps attached to a travelling carriage, while what may be called the piercing instruments worked vertically from above, the one for an awl, perforating the hole, which is entered at the succeeding stitch by the needle carrying the thread. The needle is straight, but singular to say has no point, but presents the appearance of an ordinary needle with the point broken, or cut off in the centre of the eye.[2] There is a looping instrument below. The stitch produced is the ordinary chain or single thread.

'A horizontal shaft at the top of the needle and awl bars, carries a series of tappets which give motion to the vertical bars and looper below. A long pin, acting on a large rachet gives motion to a worm which actuates the carriage and with it the work upon it.'

In 1874 Wilson built a replica of the Saint machine (see Fig 2). This was only achieved with difficulty as he had to redesign several aspects of the mechanism in order to make it work. The Saint replica was exhibited at The Centennial Show, Philadelphia, in 1876 and at the Paris Exposition Universelle of 1878. In 1894 this, the most historic sewing machine of them all—albeit a late built interpretation—was donated to the Science Museum, London, where it can still be seen (see page 17).

Legend has it that by 1800, one Balthasar Krems, a hosiery worker of Mayen, Germany, worked on knitwear with a stitching machine that had an eye-pointed needle. Certainly he was using mechanical sewing by 1810, although there is some controversy as to whether the needle was hooked or eye-pointed. No attempt seems to have been made to patent the invention and Krems died in 1813, to be remembered by his machine, somewhat restored, in the Eifel-museum, Genovevaburg, and by a replica in the Deutsches Museum in Munich.

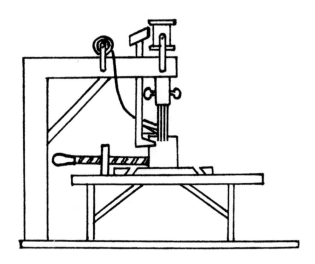

Fig 2   End view of Thomas Saint's invention patented in 1790

In the decade after 1800 there are several recorded inventions which could be termed 'sewing machines' (see Chronology, page 138). In 1814, a Viennese tailor, Joseph Madersperger, was granted an 'exclusive privilege' (patent) by the Emperor Francis I for a machine to make embroidery stitches. No commercial use seems to have been made of this invention and Madersperger waited twenty-five years before applying for a patent for his second machine. This 1839 invention had a number of eye-pointed needles that entered the cloth from below and left loops of thread when withdrawn. Through these loops a second thread was passed, twisting two stitches together to form a type of lock-stitch. The machine is now in the Technisches Museum für Industrie und Gewerbe, Vienna. Madersperger failed to exploit it commercially and died in poverty.

There is a persistent, but unverified story, that the first attempt at mechanical sewing in the USA was a machine built at Monkton, Vermont, in 1818. Grace R. Cooper's book, *The Invention of the Sewing Machine*, refers to the inclusion of this machine in the 1867 edition of *Eighty Years of Progress in the United States*—the machine was not mentioned in an earlier edition. It is stated that the machine was invented by one John Knowles who used a two-pointed needle with an eye in the middle to form a single back-stitch, such as is used in hand sewing. The source of this information is not given. Mrs Cooper also quotes John P. Stambaugh's *A History of the Sewing Machine* (1872) and the *Sewing Machine News* (July 1880) which states that two men named Adam and Dodge were responsible for the machine. Other sources mention a Rev John Adam Dodge and a mechanic, John Knowles.

The next step towards mechanical sewing occurs again in America where, on 10 March 1826, Henry Lye was granted a patent covering a machine for 'sewing leather'. No description of this machine has survived and it has been suggested that it may have comprised only a mechanical awl for making holes in leather for hand-stitching.

In the 1820s also, Barthelemy Thimonnier, a struggling tailor at St Etienne, France, was obsessed by the idea of a sewing machine and, for four years, he was almost wholly engaged in making a workable machine. By 1829 he had completed his machine which made a chain-stitch employing a barbed needle like a crochet hook. The needle was held vertically from an overhanging arm and was forced through the cloth laid horizontally. Thread was caught under the cloth and brought in a loop to the upper surface. The loops so formed were linked to make a chain-stitch. On 17 July 1830 a French patent was granted to Thimonnier and a tutor at the École des Mines, St Etienne, named Ferrand, who had assisted with the financing of the project (see page 17).

In 1841 Thimonnier was appointed to a senior position in a large Paris clothing factory engaged in the production of French army uniforms. He became subject to increasing hostility from tailors who considered the sewing machine as a threat to their livelihood.

At a time when there were eighty machines working at the factory, an angry mob of hand-sewers broke in and smashed the machines, Thimonnier barely escaping with his life. He was forced to put his machine on show as a curiosity in order to avoid starvation and tried to sell some of his hand-built machines for the equivalent of about £2.50.

Yet, by 1845, Thimonnier had produced a machine that could sew at the rate of 200 stitches per minute. He formed a partnership with Jean-Marie Magnin and together they set up a factory to build machines commercially.

On 21 February 1848, Thimonnier's world was shattered for the second time, when the revolution broke out that was to lead, four days later, to the abdication of Louis Philippe 'King of the French'. Just why the declaration of a republic should close a sewing machine factory is not clear, nor is it known if Thimonnier machines were sold commercially, but if they were, none are known to have survived. Thimonnier and Magnin were granted a British patent in 1848 and, in 1850, a US patent. Nothing was to become of these protections and Thimonnier died in poverty in 1857 at the age of sixty-four.

While Thimonnier in France was fighting misfortune, Walter Hunt, a Quaker of New York City, was aiming at a mechanical stitching device. Hunt invented a greater number of original devices than any other known American of his time, including a knife sharpener, gong bells, a yarn-twister, spinning machine, the first stove to burn hard coal, machinery for making nails and rivets, ice ploughs, velocipedes, a revolver, a repeating rifle, metallic cartridges, conical bullets, paraffin candles, a street-sweeping machine, a students' lamp, paper collars and an improved safety pin!

From 1832–4, Hunt, assisted by his brother Adoniram, had a workshop on Amos Street, New York, where Walter built a lock-stitch machine for 'sewing, stitching and seaming cloth'. The stitch used two threads, one passing through a loop in the other, and interlocking. The machine used an eye-pointed needle, moved by a vibrating arm, working in combination with a shuttle. Then, in 1834, a half-share interest in the machine was sold to George A.

Arrowsmith, owner of the Globe Stove Works, New York City. Intrigued by the invention, Arrowsmith later bought the other half interest. Hunt agreed to continue working on the machine and to prepare drawings for the patent application, but Arrowsmith was going through a period of financial difficulties and this, coupled with doubts about the morality of producing a machine which might put hand-sewers out of work, discouraged him from proceeding with manufacture, and even from patenting the invention. Hunt then lost interest as, by this time, he was engaged in new and, to him, more interesting projects.

Several patents were granted between 1840 and 1844 which had no commercial application. These included English inventors, Edward Newton and Thomas Archbold's 1841 patent for 'improvements in producing ornamental or tambour work in the manufacture of gloves', and John J. Greenough's US patent of 1842 for a mechanism to make either a running-stitch or a back-stitch, the first US patent to be issued to cover a machine specifically intended for sewing.

In March 1843, Benjamin W. Bean was granted the second American sewing machine patent. The stitch, like one of Greenough's, was a running-stitch with the material being moved between the teeth of gears. The needle, irregularly shaped but with a point at one end and an eye at the other, was held between the gears and the material was forced on to the needle. Later US and British patentees made improvements on this principle and, in 1849, Bean was granted an extension to his patent.

John Fisher and James Gibbons received British patent 10,424 on 7 December 1844. Although specified as an ornamenting device for lace, net and other fabrics, their machine featured a number of innovations to make a two-thread stitch with an eye-pointed needle and a shuttle—the first known machine to use this combination. Several sets of needles and shuttles were employed. The needles were curved in the form of a bow and were operated from under the fabric. The shuttles, pointed at both ends, were activated by two vibrating arms worked by cams. Almost every embroidery design could be produced, and though there is no record of the machine's being put to commercial use it had a far-reaching influence on future English sewing machine designs.

The most notable event of 1844, however, was the completion of a working sewing machine by Elias Howe Jr. Son of a farmer at Spencer, Massachusetts, Elias had grown up with machines from an early age. After an incomplete apprenticeship in a cotton machinery factory, he took employment with Ari Davis, a mechanic in Boston. Here, in 1839, he first heard of such a contrivance as a sewing machine.

In 1843, with an extremely low wage, a wife and three children, Howe felt driven to make an attempt to build a sewing machine which he believed would bring him a fortune. After months of watching his wife sewing, he tried to copy the movements of the human fingers but abandoned this approach in favour of a two-thread machine using a shuttle. By October 1844 he had completed a rough model that convinced him he was on the right lines. Giving up work as a journeyman mechanic, he set up a workshop with a few tools and a lathe in a small room in his father's house. A partnership was formed with an old school friend, George Fisher, under which Fisher provided lodging for Howe and his family and put up $500 in cash for tools and materials, in exchange for a half share of the patent, if granted.

During the winter of 1844 and spring of 1845 Howe worked day and night. By April he had successfully sewn a seam. By July two suits had been made on the machine, one for Fisher and the other for Howe himself. With almost uncontrollable enthusiasm he took the machine (see page 18) to the Quincy Hall Clothing Manufactory at Boston and offered to demonstrate the practicality of his invention. At the end of two weeks of critical examination, Howe challenged five of the most efficient seamstresses in the factory to compete against his machine—one seam for each of the girls and five for the machine. He finished the five seams a little sooner than the girls had completed their one.

Despite this convincing demonstration, no order was forthcoming. The reasons given were various and will be familiar to anyone who has tried to sell an invention of any kind to a potential user. It would throw the hand-sewers out of work! It would not make the whole garment! The cost was too high as thirty or forty machines would be needed!

Not discouraged, Howe set about building a second model in order to have one to deposit at the Patent Office with his application —as required by US law at that time. On 10 September 1846 patent no 4,750 was granted.[3]

George Fisher was by now having serious doubts. Boarding the Howe family and financing the invention had cost him, over two years, nearly $2,000 and still there seemed no hope of any profit. The partnership was therefore dissolved and the Howe family moved back to his father's home. With a loan from the long-suffering parent, Elias built a third machine in the hope of persuading some manufacturer in Europe to accept his invention.

Then, with yet another loan from Mr Howe Sr, machine no 3 was taken by Elias's younger brother, Amasa, to London, where contact was made with William Frederick Thomas of Cheapside, a manufacturer of corsets, umbrellas, valises and shoes, who agreed to buy the machine for £250 and to engage Elias, at £3 per week, to adapt it for making corsets. In addition, Thomas was to patent the machine in London and agreed to pay Howe £3 for every machine sold under British patent.

Although disappointed with the terms of the proposition, Elias was pleased that his machine had been accepted at last and set sail for London. Perhaps there was a clash of personalities or perhaps, as has been said, Thomas made conditions intolerable, but Howe left the job after only eight months. A fourth machine was then built which aroused little interest and only exchanged hands for an IOU of £5. The identity of the purchaser, or what became of the machine, is not known.[4]

By now Howe knew there was no future for him in England and, by pawning machine no 1—later redeemed to be used as evidence in his famous law cases—he paid for a steerage passage home. Landing in 1849 he discovered that other American inventors had been more successful in finding a market for sewing machines— indeed there were a number in daily use in Boston clothing factories, all of which appeared largely influenced by Howe's invention.

Certainly 1849 was rich in sewing machine development. In that year, Charles Morey and Joseph B. Johnson were granted US patent 6,099 for a chain-stitch machine using an eye-pointed needle. The cloth was held in place by a baster plate in a like manner to the Howe machine. Manufacture was by Safford & Williams of Boston. Two improvements to this machine were patented in the same year; one by Jotham S. Conant for a device to keep the cloth taut, and the other by John Bachelder for a method of continuous feed.

On 2 October 1849, Sherburne C. Blodgett and John A. Lerow were issued with a patent for a lock-stitch machine with a continuous shuttle movement which revolved in a circle. The 'new Rotary Sewing Machine', as it was called, was built by various manufacturers from 1849, including Orson C. Phelps in Boston, A. Bartholf, New York, and Goddard, Rice & Company, Worcester, Massachusetts.

There were no years of more importance to the development of the sewing machine than 1850 and 1851. At Boston in September 1850 the Massachusetts Charitable Mechanics Association Exhibition was staged—a silver medal going to the machine of Blodgett & Lerow, and a bronze medal to a then unknown but able inventor by the name of Allen Benjamin Wilson.

Wilson was a twenty-year-old journeyman cabinet-maker when, in 1847, he first had the idea of building a sewing machine. By 1848 the basic principles had been formulated for a lock-stitch machine using a shuttle with points at both ends to form a stitch on both forward and backward motions, by passing through a loop in the thread which had been carried by the needle through the cloth from above. After making an application for his patent, Wilson was told that his invention was an infringement of the patent of the Bradshaw machine. This groundless accusation, meant to scare Wilson off further development, led him to accept an offer from A. P. Kline and Edward Lee in which he retained only the rights for sale of the machine in New Jersey and Massachusetts.

In fact, no money was forthcoming from Kline and Lee (who operated as E. Lee & Co), but fortunately Wilson then managed to impress one Nathaniel Wheeler who contracted with E. Lee & Co to build 500 Wilson sewing machines and engaged the inventor to work on them. The two enterprising men then joined forces with partners, Warren and Woodruff, to form Wheeler, Wilson & Company. The machine built by the new company used a rotary hook and reciprocating bobbin and, to avoid litigation which might have arisen over the use of this bobbin, Wilson set about developing the stationary bobbin (US patent, 15 June 1852).

Wilson and his wife demonstrated their machine to O. E. Winchester—later to form the Winchester Repeating Arms Company—who agreed to use the machines in his shirt factory. With such a recommendation a number of factories were soon installing Wheeler & Wilson machines, and from that time the company was on a sound footing. Indeed, the Wheeler & Wilson Manufacturing Company, as it was later named, was the foremost producer of sewing machines in the US until 1870 (see page 54).

The year 1850 was also the year in which Elias Howe brought his famous infringement of patent suits against other manufacturers—an act that was to take him literally from rags to riches. Many makers of sewing machines gave in to Howe's demands, but there was one man who put up resolute opposition—a man by the name of Isaac Merritt Singer.

Notes for this chapter will be found on page 162.

3

AN INDUSTRY IS BORN

Isaac Merritt Singer was born at Pittstown, New York, on 27 October 1811, the eighth son of German immigrants. Trained as a mechanic and cabinet-maker, at an early age he was attracted to the theatrical life, becoming an actor under the name of Isaac Merritt. With $2,000 capital from the patent rights of his first invention—an excavator—he set up a theatrical company called The Merritt Players, but the troupe was soon without funds, stranded in Ohio.

Singer then took a job with a Fredericksburg manufacturer, making wooden type for printers. A New York publisher, George B. Zieber, impressed by an invention of Singer, involving the carving of wooden type, advanced him the money to build another model, after the prototype had been wrecked after a boiler explosion in a New York workshop. When this second model was completed in June 1850, Singer and Zieber carried the machine to Boston for display in the workshop of Orson C. Phelps.

As mentioned earlier, this company was building Blodgett & Lerow sewing machines, and it was in the O. C. Phelps workshop that Singer first contemplated a device of this kind. Critical of what he considered to be clumsy working, Singer was convinced that he could improve on the design. Phelps assured him that if he could substantiate this claim he would make a great deal more money from it than from the type-carving machine.

What happened next is best told in Singer's own words from a statement in a later litigation suit:

33

'I explained to them how the work was to be fed over the table and under the presser foot by a wheel having short pins on its periphery projecting through a slot in the table, so that the work would be automatically caught, fed, and freed from the pins, in place of attaching and detaching the work to and from the baster plate by hand as was necessary in the Blodgett machine.

'Phelps and Zieber were satisfied that it would work. I had no money. Zieber offered $40 to build a model machine. Phelps offered his best endeavours to carry out my plan and make the model in his shop; if successful we were to share equally. I worked at it day and night, sleeping but 3 or 4 hours out of the 24 and eating generally but once a day, as I knew I must make it for the $40 or not get it all.

'The machine was completed in 11 days. About 9 o'clock in the evening we got the parts together and tried it; it did not sew; the workmen exhausted with almost unremitting work, pronounced it a failure and left me one by one.

'Zieber held the lamp, and I continued to try the machine, but anxiety and incessant work had made me nervous and I could not get tight stitches. Sick at heart, about midnight, we started for our hotel. On the way we sat down on a pile of boards, and Zieber mentioned that the loose loops were on the upper side of the cloth.

'It flashed upon me that we had forgot to adjust the tension on the needle thread. We went back, adjusted the tension, tried the machine, sewed five stitches perfectly and the thread snapped, but that was enough. At 3 o'clock the next day the machine was finished. I took it to New York and employed Mr Charles M. Keller to patent it.'

The application for a patent was made in the names of Singer and Phelps sometime between the completion of the first prototype —September 1850—and 14 March 1851. The patent, no 8,294, was not granted until 12 August 1851 and there remains a mystery as to why the proceedings should have taken so long. One explanation could be that Singer abandoned his first application—in December 1850 he bought out Phelps's interest in the machine and may have thought it advisable to delay matters. Production did not wait for the granting of the patent, machines being made in 1850 and early 1851. The patent model, now in the collection of the Smithsonian Institution, Washington, DC, is a production model, and carries the serial number 22. The fate of Singer's prototype

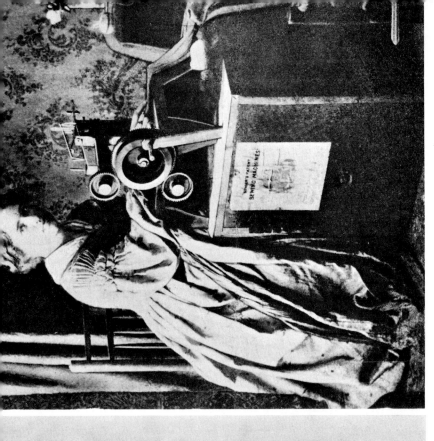

Page 35 (*left*) One of the original lock-stitch machines built by I. M. Singer in 1851; (*right*) Singer's early machine in action. Note how the housewife utilises the packing case as a sewing table

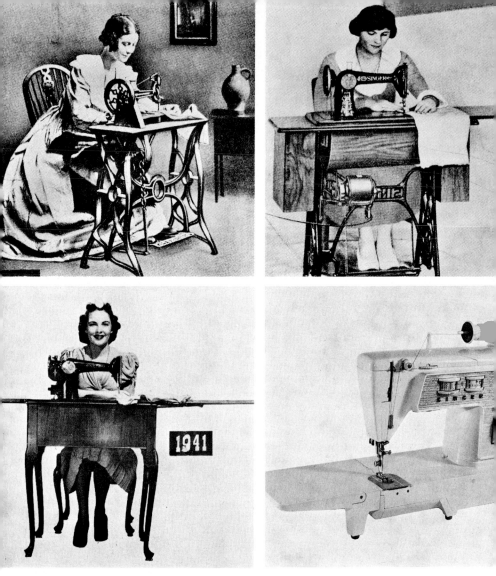

Page 36 Four stages in Singer development: (*top left*) by 1859 the treadle ensured faster sewing; (*top right*) in 1911 a motor drives the treadle and a cabinet holds the sewing aids; (*bottom left*) the 'new look' of 1941 complete with electric motor and neat cabinet to fit in with home decor; (*bottom right*) a 1970s stream-lined model with many automatic features, including a self-winding button

remains a mystery; it may have been destroyed in a fire at the Patents Office in 1877, when about 76,000 patent models were lost.

The first heavy sewing machine of I. M. Singer was to be called the Jenny Lind, after the famous Swedish singer. It may have been first advertised under that name, but it was soon changed to Singer's Perpendicular Action Sewing Machine or, more simply, the Singer Sewing Machine (see page 35 and Fig 3). A showman by nature Singer thoroughly enjoyed demonstrating the machine in public, and even exhibited it at circuses. For these demonstrations he evolved a packing case which doubled as a treadle base—a method of drive that was to be extensively used until electric power was adopted.

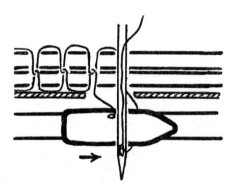

Fig 3   Lock-stitch formed by a shuttle passing through a loop of thread which is carried through the two pieces of cloth by an eye-pointed perpendicular needle. (Patented by Isaac M. Singer, 12 August 1851)

Elias Howe was by now on the track of those whom he considered had stolen the glory and profits that rightly should have been his, his legal activities being backed by George W. Bliss, partner in the Boston company of Nichols & Bliss, who built Howe patent machines. His claim against Singer was for $25,000, but payment was declined. Into the picture entered a New York lawyer, Edward Clark, who soon became Singer's partner, the two of them buying out George B. Zieber. As a defence against Howe's claims, Singer and Clark in 1853, commissioned Walter Hunt to build a replica of the sewing machine he had invented twenty years before, and submitted this with a plea that Hunt's machine had anticipated that of Howe. Then Howe sued three clothing manufacturers who were using Singer machines, and won, which gave an advantage to those who were making and selling machines under Howe's licence. Singer and Clark saw that they were beaten, paid Howe $15,000 as royalties up to July 1854, and took out a licence in line with other makers.

Singer's machines were now improved by the acquisition of the Morey & Johnson (yielding presser foot) and Bachelder (yielding presser bar) patents. The company's selling methods were well ahead of their times, with luxury showrooms and the introduction, in 1856, of Clark's idea of hire purchase—the first instance of a product to be sold under such a scheme.

United States sewing machine production in 1853 could not yet be considered extensive:

American Magnetic Sewing Machine Company (established in 1853) —about 40 machines.
Abraham Bartholf (making Blodgett & Lerow machines, under licence from Elias Howe)—135 machines.
Grover & Baker Sewing Machine Company, under licence from Elias Howe—657 machines.
Nehemiah Hunt (making machines to Christopher Hodgins's 1852 patent)—about 100 machines.
Nichols & Bliss, under licence from Elias Howe (Howe's patent)—28 machines.
I. M. Singer—810 machines.
Wheeler, Wilson Company, under licence from Elias Howe—799 machines.

Other US sewing machine manufacturing companies established by 1853 included: John P. Bowker, Boston, Massachusetts; Butterfield & Stevens, Boston, Massachusetts; Charles A. Durgin, New

York; F. R. Robinson, Boston; Waterbury Company, Waterbury, Connecticut; and Woolridge, Keene & Moore, Lynn, Massachusetts under licence from Elias Howe.

European sewing machine production of the early 1850s was less intense and taken less seriously. For instance, in 1851, at the Great Universal Exhibition in London, where several sewing machines were displayed in the Crystal Palace, Thimonnier's machine (exhibited under the name of Magnin) was overlooked, not only by the judges but by the British press which also gave no mention to the other machines on show, including a Morey & Johnson and a British Judkins (see Fig 4).

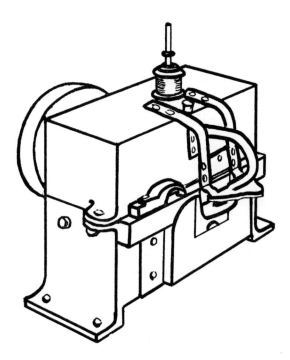

Fig 4   A Judkins machine of 1851 as displayed at the Great Exhibition, London. The machine, intended to be belt-driven in industrial use, was capable of 500 stitches per minute

A reporter from the Italian newspaper *Giornale di Roma* did, however, stumble across one of the machines and wrote: 'A little further on, you stop before a small brass machine, about the size of a quart pot, you fancy it is a meat roaster; not at all. Ha! Ha! It is a tailor! Yes a veritable stitcher. Present a piece of cloth to it; suddenly it becomes agitated, it twists about, screams audibly—a pair of scissors are projected forth—the cloth is cut; a needle set to work; and lo and behold, the process of sewing goes on with feverish activity, and before you have taken three steps a pair of inexpressibles are thrown to your feet, and the impatient machine, all fretting and fuming, seems to expect a second piece of cloth at your hands. Take care, however, as you pass along, that this most industrious of all possible machines does not lay hold of your cloak or greatcoat; if it touches even the hem of the garment it is enough—it is appropriated, the scissors are whipped out, and with its accustomed intelligence the machine sets to work, and in a twinkling another pair is produced of that article of attire, for which the English have as yet been unable to discover no name in their most comprehensive vocabulary.'

In 1852, the Oldham, Lancashire, manufacturing concern of Bradbury & Company was founded to make sewing machines, among other products, thereby laying claim to be Europe's pioneer manufacturer in this field—if one discounts Thimonnier's abortive effort to establish a sewing machine factory in 1845. Bradbury built machines under their own name, as well as that of Wellington, after the name of their works, and 'Soeze'—which speaks for itself—until the early 1900s (see Fig 14).

The year 1852 also saw the establishment of 'Symon's Patent' with premises in George Street, Blackfriars. Up to the time this chapter is written all that can be ascertained about this concern is that they advertised in 1868 that they marketed a machine called the Gem. It seems unlikely that this was related to a running-stitch machine of American manufacture in 1862 called the Little Gem.

Then, in 1853, William Frederick Thomas, of Cheapside, London, patented and started selling a lock-stitch machine. This was the Thomas who had purchased Howe's no 3 machine, with the right to British patent, in 1847. And, in America, in the same year, Amasa Howe (Elias's younger brother who had taken the no 3 machine to England in those early struggling days and carried on the negotiations with Thomas), was granted a licence to manufacture, setting up the Howe Sewing Machine Company, New York, in 1853 or 1854. Amasa built machines of very good quality and, in 1862, was awarded the highest award for sewing machines at the London International Exhibition.

Elias Howe, himself, had not manufactured sewing machines— apart from some one-off machines for clothing makers—after his return to New York in 1849, but after the success of Amasa's products he set about building a plant at Bridgeport, Connecticut, to make versions of these same machines. The Bridgeport machines were not comparable in standard to those built in New York. Amasa objected and took the matter to court, gaining an order to stop Elias trading in the company's name. The older brother then renamed his firm the Howe Machine Company—dropping the word *Sewing*. (When Elias died in 1867, the Bridgeport factory passed to his sons-in-law, the Stockwell Brothers, who also bought, in 1872, the New York company, then run by Amasa's son. Production of Howe machines was continued by the Stockwell Brothers until 1886.)

The 1854 verdict of Judge Sprague in favour of Elias Howe against I. M. Singer was followed by further verdicts against Wheeler & Wilson, Grover & Baker and other companies who were judged to be infringers of Howe's patent. This put Howe in absolute control and in receipt of a fixed royalty of $25 for every machine made by the makers to whom he had given a licence. However, the situation was far from straightforward. It had been decided that Howe owned the rights to the grooved eye-pointed needle, but now other inventors were claiming infringements regarding their improvements and refinements. Each company was suing all the others for one reason or another. The position was decidedly complicated and the lawyers were benefiting far more than the sewing machine manufacturers.

A solution was finally found by Orlando B. Potter, president of the Grover & Baker Company, who had the idea of combining interests and pooling the patents, instead of the companies trying to drive each other out of business. Potter's scheme was adopted and the Sewing Machine Combination—which, for the years it operated, was to be the terror of the numerous unlicensed makers of sewing machines—was born in 1856. Howe insisted that at least twenty-four licences at $15 per machine be granted to manufacturers, and that he was to share equally with the other three participants in the combination—Wheeler & Wilson, Grover & Baker and I. M. Singer—in addition to a special royalty of $5 for each machine sold in the USA and $1 for each machine sold abroad. When Howe's patent was renewed in 1860, his special royalty was reduced from $5 to $1, and the combination's general licence from $15 to $7 per machine.

The combination applied only to patents and no other of the companies' interests were pooled—in fact the competition was even stronger than ever as production expanded. The most important patents in the combination pool were:

1 The combination of a grooved, eye-pointed needle and shuttle (Elias Howe. US patent 4,750 of 10 September 1846).

2 The four-motion feed mechanism (Allen B. Wilson. US patent 12,116 of 19 December 1854) (see Fig 5).

3 The continuous wheel-feed, the yielding presser foot, and the heart-shaped cam applied to moving the needle bar (Isaac M. Singer. US patent 8,294 of 12 August 1851).

4 The basic patent covering a needle moving vertically above a horizontal work plate, a yielding presser resting on the work, and a perpetual or continuous feeding device (John Bachelder. US patent 6,439 of 8 May 1849, purchased by Singer and Clark).

The Sewing Machine Combination continued to control sewing machine production in the United States until 1877, when John Bachelder's twice-extended patent—then twenty-eight years old—expired.

Sewing machines in the early days of production were large, heavy contrivances, more suited for use in factories than in the

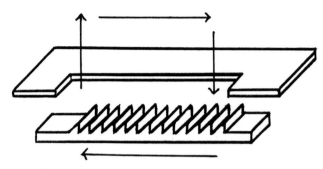

Fig 5   The almost universally adopted four-motion feed using
a serrated metal plate to give a forward movement to the cloth.
(Patented by Allen B. Wilson, 19 December 1854)

home. One man who helped set the trend for simpler, lighter and
cheaper machines was James Edward Allen Gibbs, a Virginian who had
his first taste of being a mechanic helping his father to build wool-
carding machines. In 1855 Gibbs saw a newspaper advertisement
for a Grover & Baker machine—he had not up to that time seen
an actual sewing machine. The illustration showed only the upper
part of the machine so he was at a loss to know how it could be
used to make a stitch. In Gibbs's own words: 'As I was then
living in a very out of the way place, far from railroads and public
conveyance of all kinds, modern improvements seldom reached our
locality, and not being likely to have my curiosity satisfied other-
wise, I set to work to see what I could learn from the woodcut,
which was not accompanied by any description. I first discovered
that the needle was attached to a needle arm, and consequently
could not pass entirely through the material, but must retract
through the same hole by which it entered. From this I saw that
I could not make a stitch similar to handwork, but must have some
other mode of fastening the thread on the underside, and among
other possible methods of doing this, the chain stitch occurred to
me as a likely means of accomplishing the end. I next endeavoured
to discover how the stitch was or could be made, and from the
woodcut I saw that the driving shaft which had the driving wheel

on the outer end, passed along under the cloth plate of the machine. I knew that the mechanism which made the stitch must be connected with and actuated by this driving shaft. After studying the position and relations of the needle and shaft with each other, I conceived the idea of the revolving hook on the end of the shaft, which might take hold of the thread and manipulate it into a chain-stitch. My ideas were, of course, very crude and indefinite, but it will be seen that I then had the correct conception of the invention afterwards embodied in my machine.'

It was pure curiosity which inspired Gibbs's interest in the sewing machine and he dismissed the matter from his mind until, a few months later, on a visit to his father in Rockbridge County, Virginia, he chanced upon a Singer machine working in a tailor's shop. The device greatly impressed the young man but he thought it too heavy, complicated, cumbersome, and the price ridiculously high. Strangely enough this was Singer's reaction when he saw the Blodgett machine in Phelps's Boston workshop nearly five years earlier.

Gibbs then set about in earnest to design a more functional and cheaper machine. Like many other inventors, he was encumbered by a family whose needs dictated that he had to continue working for a living. The time for his invention could only be found at night and in bad weather. Yet, by April 1856 he had progressed far enough to promote interest in his employers who offered to advance him with sufficient money to patent and develop the machine. A model was completed and Gibbs took his plans to Philadelphia to show to James Willcox who made models to accompany patent applications. The invention so impressed the model maker that he offered Gibbs the facilities of his workshop and the assistance of his son, Charles Willcox.

Patents were issued to Gibbs on 16 December 1856, 20 January 1857, and, his main one, on 2 June 1857 (see page 53). The Willcox & Gibbs Sewing Machine Company was formed in 1857, a partnership of the two Willcoxes with James Gibbs. The machine made a chain-stitch by a rotating hook and straight eye-pointed needle, the thread being looped under the work plate, and linked with the subsequent loop to form a stitch (see Figs 6 and 7). Treadle machines sold for $50 in the 1850s while competitors' machines sold at about $100. The company still exists, building industrial sewing machines.

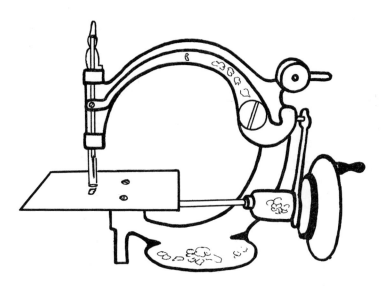

Fig 6   An 1857 Willcox & Gibbs sewing machine

James Gibbs's rationalisation of the sewing machine from a heavy factory contrivance set the trend for lighter and cheaper machines. Singer introduced the Family machine in 1858—the 'Grasshopper' as it was affectionately known in the works—but it was too light, and at $100 was overpriced. The price was reduced to $50, but still it was a poor seller. The following year Singer put the Transverse Shuttle Machine—Letter A on the market for $75. This was a considerably more successful machine and remained the company's *home* machine until 1865, when it was superseded by the New Family, a machine to be copied in most industrial countries and of a shape which was to become so familiar that many people thought a sewing machine could not look like anything else.

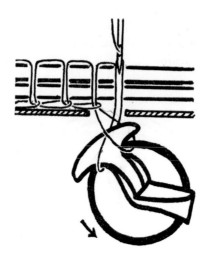

Fig 7   Chain-stitch formed by the Willcox & Gibbs rotating
hook. (Patented by James E. A. Gibbs, 2 June 1857)

In 1870, there were 69 sewing machine manufacturers listed in
the United States, producing 700,000 machines—181,260 of which
were built by Singer. By 1880 the number of manufacturers had
increased to 124 but over the next ten years had declined to 66.

Of course, it was not only in the USA that foundations for the
new industry had been laid. European inventors and manufacturers
also began producing sewing machines, though sadly, there is less
documentation of their activities.

In Germany, for instance, the Duchy of Brunswick was apparently a considerable centre of sewing machine manufacture for
many examples come to light carrying the words 'Made in Brunswick'. Notably among machines of this origin are those built for
the Atlas Machine Co of London. Various styles of lock-stitch
machines were built by this manufacturer, whose identity remains
a mystery. Among them were the Countess and Type B Atlas.
The latter machine was identical to one called the Empress,
marketed by S.D. & Co. S.D. almost certainly stood for S. Davis

who imported a machine called the Beaumont, a similar model to another Atlas importation. Were Atlas, S.D. & Co, and S. Davis one and the same company and when did they operate?

Another Brunswick-built machine was the Original Brunonia, marketed by the Alexandria (Egypt) importer, B. Segrestani. Again the machine is identical to one of the Atlas importations. One wonders how far this Brunswick manufacturer spread his commercial net.

A multitude of marques came from German factories, many machines being the factories' standard product carrying a store's or agent's name or trade mark. Almost identical models carry such names as Haid & Neu, Universum, Querida, Saxonia and Winselmann. Many examples of the work of makers such as Wertheim and Adam Opel (who later became a prominent motor car manufacturer) still survive, but details about the companies have been lost or destroyed in war or through apathy.

It is fortunate that we know something about the company of Frister & Rossmann, the famous Berlin manufacturer whose name still lives in England—the late 1960s and 1970s machines being built in Japan to English designs. What is *not* known about Frister & Rossmann is when they started to make sewing machines. The company that carries the name has two early but undated Frister & Rossmann (Berlin) machines at their warehouse in the Kent town of Swanley; one looks like a direct copy of a Willcox & Gibbs and the other, a treadle model which, until the name plate is seen, could be mistaken for a c1872 Wheeler & Wilson (see page 89). It is not known if these machines were built under licence to the American companies' specifications or if the designs were plagiarised.

In France, the country where the first sewing machine *factory* was located in 1845 (see page 140), there must have been production soon after the emergence of the new industry in America. The name 'Hurtu' was given to an early French machine but it appears that the company who produced it quickly turned its attention to motor engineering. A 'Hurtu' machine survives in the collection of Mr Henry Cassen, New York.

Detailed information about British sewing machine manufacturers of the nineteenth century, and their products, is hard to come by. Research at the Science Reference Library (formerly the Patent Office) yields some important information, but often this is on methods of unplaceable patents. Local research in libraries at centres of manufacture is usually confined to early *Kelly's Directories and Commercial Guides.*These give something of companies' histories but little about the machines themselves.

In 1859, the year Willcox & Gibbs opened their London Office, a Sheffield inventor by the name of Frederick W. Parker patented a looper which was to be used a few years later on the diminutive machine built by James Weir of Soho, London. Weir marketed his little looper machine from 1872 and possibly earlier. Certainly in 1867 he was offering The Lady's at £4.

We do know that Charles Judkins was early in the field and that he displayed a machine carrying his name at the 1851 Great Exhibition in London. This machine is now in London's Science Museum. What we do not know is the extent or duration of Judkins's production. In 1867 his machines were sold by Wonder of Ludgate Street, London.

That great patron of the sewing machine, Newton Wilson, exhibited an imported Grover & Baker in 1862, but it is not known when he started making machines under his own name at his northern factory (see page 54)

The story of the Jones sewing machine is clearer as the company still exists, now affiliated with Brother Industries. William Jones founded his factory near Manchester in 1869. At first he made both Howe and Wheeler & Wilson machines under licence. Then William, and his brother John, took out a patent to cover a machine of their own design, which went into production when the new factory opened at Guide Bridge in 1872. The Jones distinctive bentback machine of 1879 was very robust and reliable. It carried on the work plate an engraving 'as supplied to HRH The Princess of Wales', changed later, of course, to 'HM Queen Alexandra'.

Keighley, Yorkshire, was one manufacturing centre for English sewing machines—a reference of 1879 mentions the production of

10,000 machines a year in the town. The company of William Sellers, who made the Stichwell range, is said to have been founded in 1854. The list of other Keighley manufacturers taken from the 1884 *Craven's Directory* includes: Whalley, Smith & Paget, Parker Street Works, and Varley & Wolfenden, Marley Street.

Birmingham makers included Mayfield & Company, also known as the Franklin Sewing Machine Company, who built the Agenoria and Royal Franklin machines; Imperial Sewing Machine Company, Soho, built the Challenge and Imperial; Shakespeare & Illiston who operated the Royal Sewing Machine Company, Smallheath, built the Shakespeare and Royal machines; Newton Wilson of London had his factory in Birmingham; Slater & Company, Tennant Street, built the People's Sewing Machine; and a machine known as the Maxfield was made by a Birmingham manufacturer, although production dates have not yet been ascertained.

The unlikely town of Colchester in Essex was home for the Britannia Sewing Machine Company, which was established, according to *Kelly's Directories*, sometime between 1866 and 1870. In 1874 they were listed as makers of 'sewing machines of every description'. The 1888 edition does not mention sewing machines, so presumably this branch of production ceased before that date. It is believed there was another sewing machine maker in Colchester in the 1880s by the name of Aster Brothers.

In Glasgow, the ironfoundry of Kimbull & Morton built sewing machines from their establishment date in 1868 until 1955. A surviving early example of this make is cast in the shape of a lion, probably made in the 1860s or 1870s, when it was fashionable to make machines look like anything other than a functional device (see Fig 8).

While considering the early British-made sewing machines we must not forget James Starley, also known for his design and production of bicycles. Born in Albourne, Sussex, Starley started his working life on a farm. While still a youth he tramped to London and was given employment by Newton Wilson for whom he worked until 1861.

After some years Starley made a sewing machine of his own

Fig 8   A lion-headed sewing machine built by Kimbull &
Morton, Glasgow. This company was first listed as a maker of
sewing machines in 1868

design and moved to Coventry where his invention was put in
production by The Coventry Sewing Machine Company (established in 1861) for whom he acted as managing foreman. We know
from industrial histories of bicycles that, in 1868, the Coventry
Sewing Machine Company received an order to build 500[1] velocipedes for sale in France at £8 each.[2]

Starley left the company in 1869 to start making cycles in partnership with William Hillman—later founder of the Hillman Car
Company—his sewing machine interests being administered by
another partnership with Borthwick Smith.[3]

At about the time the order was received from France, the
Coventry Sewing Machine Company changed its name to the

Coventry Machinists Company and engaged several additional mechanics, among whom was one George Singer from Penn's of Greenwich, London. This Singer set up his own business in 1876 to build cycles and subsequently motor cycles (1901) and motor cars (1905). It seems an apt coincidence that a Singer, other than Isaac Merritt, should have had a connection with the sewing machine industry in its formative days.

Notes for this chapter will be found on page 162.

4

HOW AND WHAT TO COLLECT

As a beginning some collectors put cards in local shops asking for details of old sewing machines, while others buy advertising space in a newspaper. The customary places for discovering veteran machines are auctions, jumble sales and junk shops, not necessarily in that order. It is still possible to buy reasonably priced machines from auctions and second-hand shops. The more unusual and decorative machines will command the higher prices—even if the models are fairly common. A Willcox & Gibbs of late date will normally be more expensive than a Bradbury, although fewer examples of the latter make still survive. Dealers and antique shop owners, often ignorant about sewing machines, will go for the items that *look* old and interesting, aiming at resale for use as ornaments in the home.

Jumble sales are most useful. Invariably everything offered is under-valued. Runners—people who buy small antique items as cheaply as possible for resale to antique and bygone shops—make a reasonable living, simply by going through the local papers to see which church or charity is holding their sale that weekend.

When it becomes known that there is a sewing machine collector in the community, there will be no shortage of offers. Frister & Rossmanns and the ubiquitous Singers are brought to the door, sometimes seeking a good home, and occasionally to raise some cash. The author recalls his delighted surprise when a low-loader truck arrived outside the door with a Bradbury No 2 Rotary Treadle

Page 53 (*above*) James Gibbs's patent model of 1856; (*below*) Grover's patent model for the first portable sewing machine case, 1856

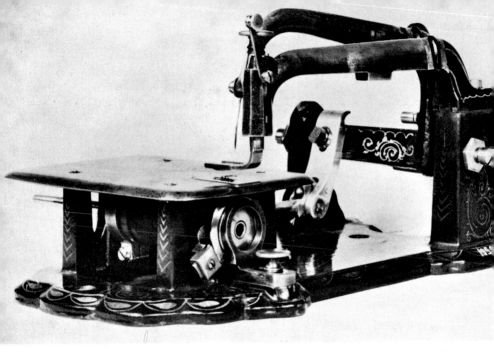

Page 54 (*above*) A Wheeler & Wilson machine employing the rotary hook and stationary bobbin and the four-motion feed invented by A. B. Wilson in 1852 and 1854; (*below*) a Newton Wilson machine

machine on board. This very heavy machine needed the assistance of a kindly neighbour to carry it into the house.

A veteran sewing machine cannot really be considered complete without an instruction book, original if possible, though a photocopy is better than nothing. Manufacturers' booklets contain more than just operating instructions or methods of threading the machine. Often a clue to the date of printing can be found either in the printing code number or in a list of awards for exhibitions. The manufacturer's address is often included, as well as those of depots. If there is an illustrated parts list, this should be compared with the actual machine—sometimes differences in design can be noted. Information of this kind can indicate that the makers simplified details in design during the course of production, or it can show that other manufacturers' methods and products have influenced the original conception.

Collectors of old sewing machines usually aim to have a selection of examples from all periods so that comparison can be made, not only between marques (see page 65) and mechanical differences, but between various styles of decoration. A machine's period of manufacture is often reflected in its ornamentation, not only the decorative ironwork but the transferred and sometimes hand-painted designs. Unless it is possible to check the serial number against a *confirmed* manufacturer's list, a periodic style of decoration is often a most useful guide to dating a particular machine. In general terms, the earlier models had floral and leafy designs, sometimes with birds and multi-coloured transfers. The last decade of the nineteenth century and the early 1900s had a typical scrolled style of decoration and, in a few cases, mother-of-pearl inlay. The 1920s decoration was angular and geometric.

In theory, a serial number, when carried, should be all that is needed to date a machine. Unfortunately, at the time this book is written, serial numbers, with a few exceptions, give very little indication as to the age of a machine. Some makes such as Frister & Rossmann used a serial number system which is incomprehensible to anyone who was not contemporarily engaged in the manufacture—many older machines of this make carry higher serial

D

numbers than machines made years later. Where information on serial numbers has been gathered, this is to be found in the Chronology in Part 2.

Where a manufacturer has ceased production, unless an agent's date list can be found, there is little chance of dating a machine by serial number. Even when a maker still exists, records have often been destroyed, particularly in Europe, where two world wars have caused an industrial historian's nightmare.

Where a patent date can be found, it is at least possible to state the earliest year when the machine could have been made. If several patent dates are shown, the later date will often indicate a modification or improvement. Then, if it is known when the particular model was dropped, it is possible to arrive at a bracket of years in which the machine was built.

Comparison with items in other collections may disclose differences in the number of patent dates carried. If a patent date of,

Fig 9   Examples of Registered Design marks. 'A' represents a design registered on 7 October 1856—7BL. The positions of the code marks were changed in 1869 to those shown in example 'B', the date in this case being 2 May 1878—2ED

say, 1884 is carried on one machine, and the latest date shown on a second example is 1878, it is certain that the first machine was built in that six-year period. Almost certain, rather, because the machine not carrying a later refinement may have continued in production.

Registered design marks are useful where British-made machines of before 1883 are concerned. Not all machines carried this mark, but when used it sometimes takes the place of a patent date. The mark was a diamond with the letters 'Rd' in the centre. Between 1842 and 1867 a key letter for the year was carried within the top corner of the diamond. From 1868 until 1883 the key letter was carried within the right-hand corner. The key letters were coded as follows:

1842	1843	1844	1845	1846	1847	1848	1849	1850	1851
X	H	C	A	I	F	U	S	V	P

1852	1853	1854	1855	1856	1857	1858	1859	1860	1861
D	Y	J	E	L	K	B	M	Z	R

1862	1863	1864	1865	1866	1867	1868	1869	1870	1871
O	G	N	W	Q	T	X	H	O	A

1872	1873	1874	1875	1876	1877	1878	1879	1880	1881
I	F	U	S	V	P	D	Y	J	E

1882	1883
L	K

The letters and figures in the other corners of the diamond indicate the day and month of registration and the 'bundle'. The letter in a circle at the head of the diamond shows the class of goods. The month of registration had a separate code, but here we are concerned only with the year.

ATTACHMENTS

One of the most surprising aspects of the early sewing machine is the variety of work it will execute. Within a few years of evolving a stitch that could be mechanically made, inventors were putting their minds to devices that would present the work in such ways that the stitch would have a variety of applications. A look into the

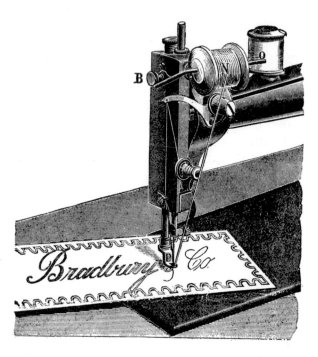

Fig 10   A braiding attachment with fix-on reel rig for use on the
Bradbury Rotary Shuttle machine

attachment box of a veteran sewing machine will disclose an array of mysterious binders, quilters, braiders, markers and guides, various presser feet for gathering, frilling and hemming, corders and edge-stitchers, and buttonholers, looking for all the world like the implements to be attached to some diminutive agricultural tractor. It is sad that in many cases the inventive genius behind these attachments was lost on the ladies who used the sewing machines when they were new, and many of these interesting accessories have stayed in their box, still slightly oiled, just as they left the factory.

The first attachment to be patented was a simple device for stitching a binding edge to the material. This was a US patent granted to Harry Sweet in 1853. The binder was followed by the hemmer which turned the material back to itself. Then came various braiders and embroiderers of which there are many interesting examples, some with a fix-on braid reel rig to attach to the upper part of the machine head. A stitching machine for making button-holes was patented in 1854 and, two years later, an attachment for fitting to a normal machine was patented, although it was not developed to a successful degree until the late 1860s.

Electric motors to drive machines were being experimented with by inventors in the 1860s, notably Solomon Jones, who was granted a US patent for such a drive in 1871. However, the electric motor had to wait until the twentieth century before being commonly adopted.

One of the most entertaining of the nineteenth-century sewing machine attachments was the musical cover, patented by George D. Garvie and George Wood in the USA in 1882. This was a player-piano type of instrument operated by the machine's treadle. 'Will play any tune—Can be played by anyone' went the advertising slogan. Another rather frivolous attachment was C. D. Stewart's patented fanning attachment which was made in the USA by James Morrison & Company.

Thread reels have been made in a diversity of forms and sizes, some even being fashioned from ivory. The manufacture of cotton thread as an industry originated in Paisley, Scotland, at the time of the Napoleonic wars and the resultant sea blockade which restricted the British importation of silk. Heddle strings for looms were made from silk and a substitute had to be found. A successful three-ply cotton thread was developed by the brothers James and Patrick Clark of Paisley. By 1820 two factories were making cotton thread: J. & J. Clark & Company, run by the sons of the inventors, and J. & P. Coats & Company of Ferguslie—a factory established in 1815. However, three-ply cotton thread was not altogether satisfactory for mechanical sewing; linen thread was too coarse and silk too expensive.

Improvements in the processing of cotton thread were made and, in 1850, C. E. Bennett of Portsmouth, New Hampshire, USA, produced a six-ply thread for which he was granted a gold medal at the Fair of the American Institute. Still the thread was wiry and glazed, and it was not until the mid-1860s that a satisfactory cotton thread for machine use had been developed, manufactured by George A. Clark and William Clark of Newark, New Jersey—descendants of the Paisley Clarks. At the Newark mill, the Clarks produced a six-cord cable thread, made up of three two-ply yarns. This was named Our New Thread or ONT for short (see Fig 11). J. & P. Coats used the description 'Best Six-Cord', and Willimantic called theirs the 'Superior Six-cord' cotton thread.

Fig 11   Six-cord cable cotton thread introduced in the 1860s by George A. Clark and William Clark and known as Clarks's Our New Thread, shortened later to ONT

RESTORATION

The basic rule in restoration is to do as little as possible and to keep disturbance of the original work to a minimum. In common with most mechanical bygones, veteran sewing machines quickly respond to cleaning and oiling and, in many cases, this is all that is necessary to put a machine in a condition to be included in a collection.

When a machine is very dirty or badly rusted it is best, after a general cleaning, to attend to each individual component, first removing the part. Sometimes a freeing agent or easing oil is needed on parts which are intended to move but do not. In most cases screws will respond to an overnight impregnation by a freeing agent. Rusted 'bright' metal should be treated with a rust remover, and the areas which do not clean off can be given extra attention with extremely fine emery paper.

The choice of cleaning and polishing materials is a matter of personal selection; everyone will have their own ideas on the best products to use. Plated parts may be cleaned first with a chrome cleaner and then with silver polish. Some collectors go beyond this modest treatment and resort to re-plating which is an expensive process and not truly satisfactory. The plating applied to early sewing machines was nickel and, being of a different hue, a chrome deposit will look out of place.

Much of a veteran machine's interest lies in its decoration and laquerwork which can be brought back to life with wax polish. On no account should a machine be repainted as this, to a large extent, destroys its historical value. Transfers should not be retouched unless the work is carried out by a very able restorer.

PART 2

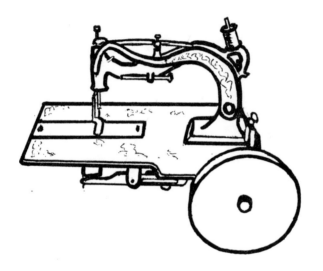

DIRECTORY OF MARQUES, INVENTORS AND MANUFACTURERS

It cannot be claimed that the following list is a comprehensive survey of all the names connected with the long and complex history of the sewing machine. Hitherto unknown makes are continually coming to light and even while this book is being prepared, additions and corrections are being made. However, the Directory will be useful to collectors when tracing histories of machines.

The author is anxious to have further information about the marques and manufacturers listed as well as about those which have not been covered.

Acme   The name used for machines built by the Highby Sewing Machine Company, Brattleboro, Vermont. The company was in production from c1882 until after 1886.

Adam Opel   Manufacturer of the Titania and probably a machine known as the Nelson. This German factory exists today as an important motor vehicle manufacturer. Production dates of sewing machines not known, but motor production started in 1898 with the acquisition of the rights to build the Lutzmann car.

Adjustable Belgravia   According to an early advertisement, this was an improved Wheeler & Wilson machine with the patent date of 1868. The distributor's address was 20 High Holborn, London.

Advance Premier   Marketed by J. Theobold & Company, 43 Farringdon Road, London. Advertised in 1893 at 15 shillings.

Aetna   Made by the Aetna Sewing Machine Company, Lowell, Mass, USA, between c1867 and c1877.

Agenoria   One of the marques made by the Franklin Sewing Machine Company, Birmingham, England. Production began about 1868. In June of that year an Agenoria was purchased carrying the serial number '373'. In the 1870s, S. Smith & Company, Soho Bazaar, London, were offering the Agenoria lockstitch machine at £4 4s. This machine bore a striking resemblance to one marketed by Newton Wilson. Another machine built by the same factory was known as the Royal Franklin. One surviving machine is marked Mayfield & Company, Agenoria Works, Birmingham; it also carries the designation 'R4'.

Aiken & Felthousen   Very little is known about this maker except that they were based at Ithaca, NY, USA, and made machines from c1855 and ceased production before 1880.

Alberta   With Excelsior, this was a machine marketed by White (or Whight—alternative spelling found in some sources) & Mann, 143 Holborn Bars, London. In 1868 the machines ranged in price from £6 to £12 12s.

Alexandra   Origin not known. In the 1870s, S. Smith & Company, Soho Bazaar, London, were offering the machine at £9 9s.

Alsop   An American make that disappeared from the market about 1880.

American   A machine of the American Sewing Machine Company in the USA. Production was started in 1854. It is not known if the company was associated with other machines of this name.

American   Marketed by the American Sewing Machine Company, London, who also sold the Saxonia. This American was very like the Willcox & Gibbs machine in appearance.

American   A chain-stitch machine marketed by James Weir. In 1867 it was priced at £2 15s.

American Buttonhole, Overseaming & Sewing Machine Between 1869 and about 1874 this machine was built by the company of the same name in Philadelphia, USA. From c1874 until c1886 the machine was known as the New American and built by the American Sewing Machine Company, Philadelphia. In 1868 Newton Wilson sold this machine in London.

American Domestic (also known as the Little Domestic)   A machine marketed by Gordon & Gotch, 15 St Bride Street, London. In the 1880s it was priced at £4 4s.

American Hand Sewing Machine Company, Bridgeport, Conn, USA   Makers of Sewing Shears between c1884 and c1900. This type of sewing appliance was the invention of Joseph Hendrick whose US patent model was dated 1858.

American Magnetic   Built by the American Magnetic Sewing Machine Company, Ithaca, NY, USA, in the years 1853 and 1854. Only one example of the make is known to exist—in the collection of the Northern Indiana Historical Society.

Anchor   Alternative name for Royal Anchor and Shuttle Anchor, made in Manchester and marketed by Thomas Bradford & Company, London. Production dates are not known but the machine was advertised in 1871.

Andrews, William, Birmingham, England   Maker of sewing machines in the 1860s. One of Andrews's productions was called the Sanspareil.

Archbold, Thomas   Granted British patent in 1841 in association with Edward Newton. The machine was for tambouring or ornamenting the backs of gloves.

Arrowsmith, George A.   Purchased Walter Hunt's sewing machine with rights to patent.

Aster Brothers, Colchester   Makers of sewing machines in the 1880s.

Atlantic A machine based on the patent of L. Porter and Alonzo Porter. The machine was built in the USA for a short period in the 1870s (see Fig 12).

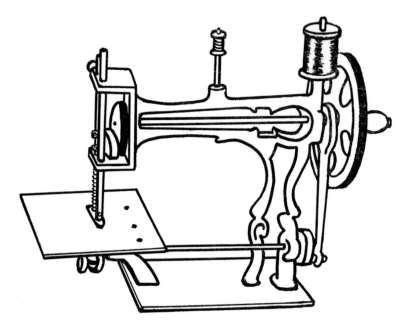

Fig 12   The 1869 Atlantic sewing machine. One of the many short-lived productions that were built in the 1860s and 1870s

Atlas Marketed by the Atlas Machine Company, 88 High Street, Camden Town, London. Dates of the company's operation have not been ascertained. The sewing machine range included the Countess. The Type B Atlas (made in Brunswick) is identical to the Empress marketed by S.D. & Co (probably standing for S. Davis & Company), London, and it is likely that these companies were linked.

68

Atwater   A design patented by B. Atwater, USA. The machine was produced between 1857 and about 1860.

Avery   A product of the Avery Sewing Machine Company, New York, in the 1850s.

Avery   Made by the Avery Manufacturing Company, New York. Production is said to have started in 1875 and to have lasted until after 1936.

Babcock   An American sewing machine. No production dates available.

Bachelder, John   American inventor who patented improvements to the Morey & Johnson machine in 1849.

Bacon & Company, G. W., London, England   This name appeared on some Beckwith machines when sold in England.

Baker, William E.   See Grover & Baker.

Baker, Isaac F.   The patentee of The Lady sewing machine, built in the USA around the year 1859. The head of the machine was cast in the form of a figure depicting Cora Munro, a character from James Fenimore Cooper's book, *The Last of the Mohicans*.

Banner   An American make. Production dates unknown.

Barker, Samuel   With Thomas White, Barker was the manufacturer of the Brattleboro machine at Brattleboro, Vermont, from c1858 until 1861.

Barlow & Son   Manufacturers of the simple Beckwith machine in New York in 1871 and 1872.

Bartholf, Abraham, New York   Maker of the Blodgett & Lerow machine from 1850 for a very short period. From 1853 until c1856 a machine based on the 1846 patent of Elias Howe was built. After 1856 machines of other designs were made. From 1859 this manufacturer was known as the Bartholf Sewing Machine Company, ceasing production about 1865.

Bartlett The design of Joseph W. Bartlett, built between 1866 and c1870 by Goodspeed & Wyman Sewing Machine Company, USA. From c1870 until 1872 the machine was built by the Bartlett Sewing Machine Company, New York. Bartlett later went on to build street lamps. Superficially the Bartlett resembles the design of Willcox & Gibbs but the action is entirely different.

Bartram & Fanton Built by the Bartram & Fanton Manufacturing Company, Danbury, Conn, USA, between 1867 and 1874, under the patents of W. B. Bartram (see Fig 13).

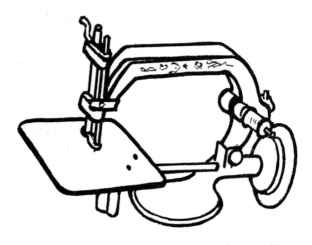

Fig 13 1867 Bartram & Fanton sewing machine

Bay State An obscure American marque which disappeared before 1880.

Bean, Benjamin W. American inventor granted a sewing machine patent in 1843.

Beane, John W. American manufacturer producing sewing machines in the 1850s.

Beans No particulars known.

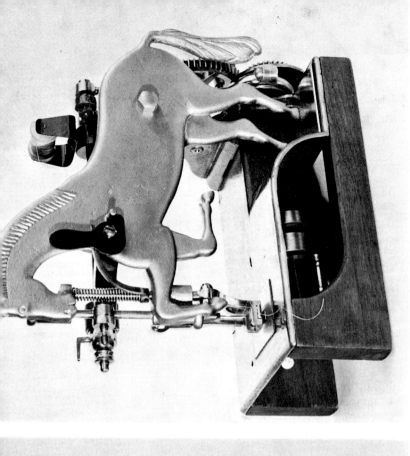

Page 71 1858 produced some startling patents including (*left*) Hendrick's sewing shears, and (*right*) the horse machine of Perry

Page 72 (*above*) A James Weir chain-stitch machine, probably from the 1870s; (*below*) a c1870 Shakespeare, carrying the serial number 35245

Beaumont   A German-built machine built for S. Davis & Company. The design is identical to a machine marketed by the Atlas Machine Company, Camden Town, London.

Beckwith   A simple sewing machine which operated like a spring-loaded stapler, invented by William G. Beckwith and built in 1871 and 1872 by Barlow & Son, New York. After 1872 and up to c1876 the name of the manufacturer was Beckwith Sewing Machine Company, New York. In the 1870s, S. Smith & Company, Soho Bazaar, London, were offering the Beckwith at £2 2s. A surviving example is engraved 'G. W. Bacon & Company, London, England'—he was probably the man who imported the machines.

Beetham of Leeds   Manufacturer or sales outlet for the Dolly Varden sewing machine.

Belgravia   See Adjustable Belgravia.

Benford, E. G., 16 Castle Square, Brighton, Sussex   From 1869 agent and possibly importer of sewing machines. One example carries patent date July 1882.

Bennett   Nothing is known apart from indication that this was an American manufacturer, probably making the Pearl sewing machine from about 1859. A manufacturer by the name of Bennett, in Chicago, built the Boudoir machine during at least some of the period 1857–c1870.

Biesolt & Locke   A German make of machine produced at Weisden.

Blake's Leather Stitching Machine   Built in the USA to Lyman H. Blake's patent of 1858.

Blanchard   American marque. No particulars known.

Blees   A machine built by the Blees Sewing Machine Company, USA, between 1870 and 1873.

Bliss, George W.   As a partner in the company of Nichols & Bliss of Boston, USA, Bliss produced Howe patent machines in the year 1853.

Blodgett & Lerow   Machines resulting from the partnership of Sherburne C. Blodgett and John A. Lerow. Issued with US patent in 1849. In that year machines to this design were made by O. Phelps, Boston. Two other manufacturers were involved: Goddard, Rice & Company, Worcester, Mass (1849–50), and A. Bartholf, New York, between 1849 and sometime in the 1850s.

Bond   An American make of machine that went out of production before 1880.

Boston   Subsequently called New Boston. Production began in 1880 by J. F. Paul & Company, Boston, Mass. Later this company was known as the Boston Sewing Machine Company. Machines of this name were still being made in 1886.

Boston Star   Sold by the National Sewing Machine Company, London. No further information available.

Boudoir   A single-thread chain-stitch machine, invented by Daniel Harris, whose patents are dated 1857 and 1858. Several manufacturers are thought to have made this machine between 1857 and about 1870, including Bennett of Chicago. The machine was also known as the Harris's Patent Sewing Machine.

Bowker, John P.   Manufacturer in Boston, Mass, who built the Dorcas sewing machine from 1853. Production is thought to have ceased before 1860.

Bradbury & Company Limited, Wellington Works, Oldham, England   This company had showrooms and depts at 14 Newgate Street, and 217 Commercial Road, London. Founded in 1852 and, according to Oldham Trade Directories of c1900, were the pioneers of sewing machines in Europe. Production ceased in the early 1900s. Sewing machines under the names Bradbury, Wellington and Soeze were made. Bradburys also produced baby carriages, bicycles and, for a short period, motor cycles (see Fig 14).

74

STITCH REGULATOR.

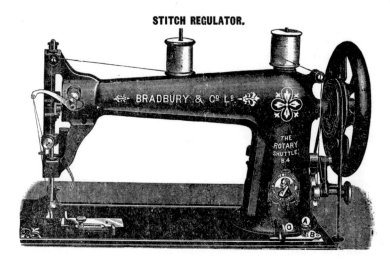

Fig 14   A Bradbury Rotary Shuttle sewing machine. This is a typical example of a late nineteenth-century European design

Bradford & Barber   Manufactured by a company of the same name in Boston, Mass, in the years 1860 and 1861.

Bradford & Company, Thomas, Manchester (works at Crescent Iron Works, Salford)   Famous iron founders who produced many items of domestic equipment. Makers of sewing machines from c1869. The name made a final appearance in a Manchester trades directory in 1894. The company's London office was at 63 Fleet Street. Thomas Bradford & Company produced the Anchor, Royal Anchor, and Shuttle Anchor machines.

Bradshaw, John A.   Granted a US patent for a sewing machine in 1848.

Brattleboro   A machine built by Samuel Barker and Thomas White, Brattleboro, Vermont, from about 1858 until 1861.

Brind, Henry   An American maker of sewing machines about 1860.

Britannia Manufacturing Company, Colchester, Essex   According to advertisements, built an *improved* Wheeler & Wilson sewing machine. Established sometime between 1866 and 1870 and made sewing machines until c1887 thereafter produced engineering tools, petroleum oil engines and later motor cycles. In the 1870s, S. Smith & Company, Soho Bazaar, London, were offering a Britannia sewing machine at £6 16s 6d.

Brown Rotary   An American sewing machine about which nothing can be traced.

Brown & Sons, Benjamin, Birmingham, England   Listed as sewing machine manufacturers in 1865.

Brown, W. N.   Granted US patent in 1859. No production models known to exist.

Buckeye   A lock-stitch shuttle machine, later known as New Buckeye and Improved Buckeye. Machines built by the W. G. Wilson Sewing Machine Company, Cleveland, Ohio, from c1867 and c1876.

Buell   Also marked 'E. T. Lathbury's Patent'. A machine built by A. B. Buell, Westmoreland, NY, from about 1860. It is not known when production ceased.

Burnet & Broderick   A short-lived make of American sewing machine which appeared in 1859.

Butterfield & Stevens Manufacturing Company, Boston, Mass   The makers of the Wickersham sewing machine from 1853.

Canada Sewing Machine Company   Purchased by R. M. Wanzer in 1878.

Canadian   Manufactured by the Gardner Sewing Machine Company, Hamilton, Ontario, Canada. Production dates unknown put certainly started prior to 1884.

Carver & Company, Birmingham, England Maker of sewing machines in the 1860s.

Castle A sewing machine of unknown origin. The L8 No 4 model is similar to the Singer vibrating shuttle machine.

Centennial A two-thread machine, made by the Centennial Sewing Machine Company, Philadelphia, between 1873 and 1876. It was based on the J. N. McLean patents of 1869 and 1870 and was similar to the McLean & Hooper machine made by B. W. Lacy & Company, Philadelphia, up to about 1873.

Challenge Built by the Imperial Sewing Machine Company, Soho, Birmingham, using the Harris & Judson patent of 1871. In the 1870s, S. Smith & Company, Soho Bazaar, London, were offering the Challenge at £4 4s.

Chamberlain This machine was built by Woolridge, Keene & Moore of Lynn, Mass, for about one year commencing in 1853.

Champion See O. Robinson & Company.

Chapman, William and Edward Walter Granted UK patent in 1807 for a machine to sew belting and rope.

Cherub A decorative sewing machine patented by American inventor T. J. W. Robertson in 1857 and made by D. W. Clark in Bridgeport, Conn. This was one of several highly ornamental machines produced by this manufacturer until the early 1860s.

Chicago Singer Built by Scates, Tryber & Sweetland Manufacturing Company, Chicago, Illinois, between the years 1879 and 1882. From 1882 until about 1885 the machine was marketed simply as the Chicago, being built by the Chicago Sewing Machine Company.

Clark D. W. Clark, Bridgeport, Conn, was making sewing machines from about 1858 until after 1860. In that period a number of designs were produced including the highly ornamented designs of T. J. W. Robertson, notably the Cherub, the Foliage and the Dolphin models.

77

Clark's Revolving Looper A two-thread machine built by Lansom, Goodnow & Yale, of Windsor, Vermont, from 1859 and 1861. It was made under the patent of 1859 issued to Edwin Clark, who had based his design on improvements to the Grover & Baker, Nettleton & Raymond, and the Windsor machines, the latter originating from the manufacturers' predecessor, the Vermont Arms Company (see Fig 15).

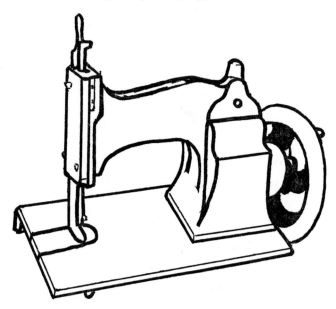

Fig 15 1860 Clark's Revolving Looper made by Lamson, Goodnow & Yale, Windsor, Vermont. A large order for arms for the Civil War halted sewing machine production and the equipment for making this and the Windsor machine was sold to Grout & White of Massachusetts

Cleopatra The name of a sewing machine marketed by Newton Wilson of Holborn, London. In 1867 this chain-stitch machine was sold at £4 4s, and it continued to be sold at this price in the 1870s.

Clinton Made by Clinton Brothers, Ithaca, New York, c1861–5.

Cochrane Company, Thomas M., Bellville, Illinois   Manufacturer of the New Fairbanks machine from 1880.

Cole   An American make. No information available.

Collier & Son, J., 136 Clapham Road, London   Marketed the Swift & Sure sewing machine. Production dates unknown. The company also marketed the Jones machine under their own name.

Companion   Made by the Thurston Manufacturing Company, Marlboro, New Hampshire, from 1882. It is not known when production ceased.

Cookson Lockstitch Sewing Machine Company Limited   Makers of a machine designed by Frederick Nesfield Cookson of Wolverhampton and Birmingham, England, who patented his invention in 1886–7.

Countess   Sold in London by the Atlas Machine Company. Presumably of German origin. No production dates known.

Coventry Sewing Machine Company, England   Makers of the European sewing machine. Established in 1861 and built sewing machines until sometime after 1870. In 1869 the name was changed to the Coventry Machinists' Company, and cycle manufacturing was commenced.

Crown   Made by the Florence Sewing Machine Company, Florence, Mass, from 1879 until after 1886. The machine was originally known as the Florence from about 1860. In 1885 the company changed its character and started to make lamps and heating stoves. The New Crown sewing machine was introduced and the right to use the name Florence was sold to a mid-western manufacturer who applied it to an entirely different design of machine. The Florence Sewing Machine Company became known as Crown Improvements about the year 1880.

Crowshaw, William, Birmingham, England   Listed as sewing machine manufacturer in 1864.

Cyprus A European-made machine similar in design to a Hand Stitchwell machine built by William Sellers & Sons, Keighley, Yorkshire.

Dale In 1863 John D. Dale was granted a US patent for a running-stitch machine. It is thought that the machine was put into commercial production but no dates are available.

Dauntless Produced by the Dauntless Manufacturing Company, Norwalk, Ohio, from 1877 until after 1882. At a late stage of manufacture the name was changed to New Dauntless. The company also made the Queen sewing machine from c1881.

Davis The Davis Sewing Machine Company, Watertown, New York, built the Davis Vertical Feed machine from 1869 until after 1886. At about this time the company moved to Dayton, Ohio and produced the Davis Vertical Feed and Davis Rotary Shuttle machines. The Defiance was also made at the Dayton works. The company ceased production in 1924. The inventor is thought to have been J. A. Davis of New York who began making machines c1860.

Davis, S. British agent or importer of the Beaumont machine. See S.D. & Co. Probably allied to the Atlas Machine Company, Camden Town.

Decker The Decker Manufacturing Company, Detroit, Mich, built this and the Princess machine for an unknown period before 1881.

Defiance Made by the Davis Sewing Machine Company, Dayton, Ohio, after, it is thought, 1886. A machine bearing the name Defiance was also made by the Standard Sewing Machine Company, Cleveland, Ohio.

Defiance N3 A foreign, presumably German-built machine of the New Family style.

Demorest Built by the Demorest Manufacturing Company between 1882 and 1908. The manufacturer was previously known as the New York Sewing Machine Company and produced machines carrying the name New York.

Demorest, Madam, New York Marketed the Fairy sewing machine based on Aaron Palmer's patent of 1862, between the years 1863 and about 1865.

Diamond The name given to the Sigwalt sewing machine from 1880. The machine was in production from c1879 up to an unknown date by the Sigwalt Sewing Machine Company, Chicago, Illinois.

Dietrich A German-built sewing machine. A company by this name built the Vesta machine.

Dodge, Rev John Adam Said to have made a sewing machine in Monkton, Vermont, in 1818 or 1819.

Dolly Varden A machine made or marketed by Beetham of Leeds.

Dolphin A highly ornamental design of American inventor, T. J. W. Robertson, in 1855 and built by D. W. Clark, Bridgeport, Conn.

Domestic William A. Mack & Company, and N. S. Perkins of Norwalk, Ohio, began sewing machine manufacture in 1864. In 1869 the makers' name was changed to the Domestic Sewing Machine Company but was still based at Norwalk. In 1924 the White Sewing Machine Company acquired the title and maintained it as a subsidiary at Cleveland, Ohio. From about 1882 the company produced the Little Giant machine. It is possible that there was a relationship with the American Domestic machine that was marketed by the London company of Gordon & Gotch in the 1880s.

Dominion or **New Dominion** No information available.

Dorcas A lock-stitch machine marketed by Newton Wilson, Holborn, London. In 1867 the price was £4 4s.

Dorcas Made by John P. Bowker, Boston, Mass, from 1853. Production had ceased by 1860.

Dorman Lockstitch Sewing Machine and Engineering Company, Northampton, England   Production dates 1890–c1900.

Drew & Company, J. H.   Makers of the New Fairbanks machine between 1878 and 1880.

Duff & Rowntree, Bishop Auckland, County Durham   Marketed the New American sewing machine.

Du Laney, G. L.   Granted US patents in 1866 and 1871 on which the Little Monitor was based. Du Laney made the machine at Brooklyn, NY, from about 1866 until after 1875.

Duncan, John   A Glasgow inventor who patented a tambouring machine in 1804.

Duplex No information available about this American make.

Durgin A machine built in the mid-1850s by Charles A. Durgin, New York.

Durkopp German-made leather stitcher. No particulars known.

Eclipse Built by Shepherd, Rothwell & Hughes, Oldham, England. Advertised in 1873 at prices ranging from £6 10s to £8 10s.

Economist An American make. No particulars available.

Eldridge Built by the Eldridge Sewing Machine Company, Chicago, between 1869 and 1890. In 1890 the company consolidated with the June Manufacturing Company, also of Chicago, to become the National Sewing Machine Company, Belvidere, Illinois. Production from this company continued until 1953.

Elgia or **Elgin** A New Family style of machine, probably made in Germany and possibly by Frister & Rossmann. Production dates not known.

Elliptic   Originally known as Sloat's Elliptic. Initially made by George B. Sloat & Company, Philadelphia from about 1858. In 1860 the company amalgamated with the Lester Manufacturing Company to become the Union Sewing Machine Company of Richmond, Virginia. The company was short-lived and between 1861 and c1867 the machine was built by the Wheeler & Wilson Manufacturing Company. In 1867 the Elliptic Sewing Machine Company, New York, was formed. The marque disappeared before 1880. In the 1870s, the Elliptic was being offered by S. Smith & Company, Soho Bazaar, London, at £7 10s.

Ellithorp & Fox   In 1857 S. B. Ellithorp was granted a patent for a two-thread, stationary-bobbin machine. It was designed in the shape of a squirrel but as no machine of this shape has been known to survive, there is speculation that perhaps the machine did not go into production. The name Fox appears on the patent rights but nothing is known about this gentleman .

Elsa   A lock-stitch machine illustrated in the London store Whiteley's catalogue of 1911. The machine was priced at £1 5s.

Emery, Houghton & Company, Boston, Mass   Makers of the Johnson machine from 1856 until after 1865.

Empire   Made by the Empire Sewing Machine Company, New York, from 1866 until c1870. It is reported that the patent for the design was granted to Stephen C. Ketchum.

Empire   Built by the Empire Company, Boston, Mass, from 1860 until 1870. Between 1870 and 1872 the machine known as the Remington Empire was produced by the Remington Empire Sewing Machine Company. In 1873, the year Remington turned attention to the manufacture of typewriters, the machine, by then called the Remington, was made by E. Remington & Sons, Philadelphia. Production ceased about 1894. Both lock-stitch and chain-stitch machines were made under this name.

Empress   A machine of German origin, marketed by S.D. & Co, London. Identical to the Brunswick-made Type B Atlas.

The slogan 'We Move With The Times' was carried on the machine. Production dates not known.

Empress Manufactured on order through Jerome B. Secor, Bridgeport, Conn, from 1877 until some unknown date.

England's Queen Origin not known. In the 1870s S. Smith & Company, Soho Bazaar, London, were offering this machine at £5 5s.

Epsonia Nothing known about this make. A No 3 model has been included in the Veteran Machine Register.

Erie An American make of machine. No particulars available.

Estey The Estey Sewing Machine Company began production about 1880. In 1883 the manufacture was undertaken by the Brattleboro Sewing Machine Company of Brattleboro, Vermont. The machine was being marketed in 1886.

Eureka Made by the Eureka Shuttle Sewing Machine Company, New York, in 1859. Only the patent model is known to survive, this machine carrying the address: 469 Broadway (see Fig 16).

Europa A machine built by Smith & Starley. No production dates are available, but it is known the machine was being sold in 1877. Similar in design to one of the Newton Wilson models.

European A machine designed by James Starley and built by the Coventry Machinists' Company.

European Sewing Machine Company, England No particulars known. 1869 is the earliest discovered date of the company's activity. Possibly part of the Coventry Machinists' Company.

Excelsior A machine built by the Excelsior Sewing Machine Company, New York, in 1854 only. A machine of this name was marketed by White (or Whight) & Mann, 143 Holborn Bars, London, in 1867, but it is not thought that this machine had any connection with the American machine. Also, an Excelsior was

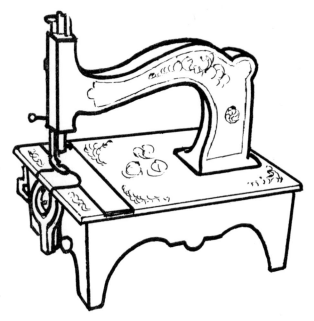

Fig 16   The 1859 Eureka sewing machine, of which no written
record can be found. The example in the Smithsonian Institution
collection is a patent model covering minor improvements in
design

being offered in the 1870s by S. Smith & Company, Soho
Bazaar, London, at £6 6s.

Express   A name possibly used by the Hamburg manufacturer,
Ghul & Harbeck. A machine called the Original Express was
built by this factory.

Express   Built in Coventry. Designed by James Starley.

Express Chainstitch   A machine that appeared in the 1911 catalogue of Whiteley's, of London. The price was 16s. It is unlikely
this machine was connected with the two marques above.

Fairy   A small running-stitch machine based on Aaron Palmer's

US patent of 1862, and marketed by Madam Demorest, New York, from 1863 to 1865.

Family Favorite One of a range of machines built in 1867 by the Weed Sewing Machine Company, Hartford, Conn

Farmer & Gardner Manufacturing Company Builders of the Wesson machine in 1879 and 1880. It was then produced by the D. B. Wesson Sewing Machine Company, Springfield, Mass

Farringdon A lock-stitch machine, probably of British make with a similar appearance to the 1879–1907 model made by William Jones, Guide Bridge, Lancashire, but carrying the letters C, J and M entwined as a motive for a trade mark.

Faudels, London No information other than the existence of the name. The machine bears a resemblance to the Singer New Family.

Finkle A lock-stitch machine built by Milton Finkle, Boston, Mass, from 1856 until c1859. About 1859 Finkle entered partnership with a man called Lyon. The machine became known as the Victor from 1867, and in 1872 the company changed its name to the Victor Sewing Machine Company, Middletown, Conn. Production ceased sometime around 1890.

First & Frost A manufacturer in New York, building machines between c1859 and c1861.

Fisher, John With James Gibbons, Fisher was granted a British patent in 1844 for a machine using an eye-pointed needle and a shuttle.

Florence Based on the patents of Leander W. Langdon, this machine was built by the Florence Sewing Machine Company, Florence, Mass, from about 1860 until after 1878. From 1879 the company's sewing machine was known as the Crown. In the 1870s, S. Smith & Company, Soho Bazaar, London, were offering the Florence at £10.

Foley & Williams Manufacturing Company, Chicago Makers of

the Goodrich machine between c1895 until c1920. Originally the machine was produced by H. B. Goodrich, Chicago.

Folsom   J. G. Folsom, Winchendon, Mass, built sewing machines from 1865 until c1871, including the Globe. In 1865 Folsom exhibited a New England machine together with his Globe machine. It is possible that both were made by him at that time.

Fosket & Savage, Meridan, Conn   Made sewing machines in 1858 and 1859.

Foxboro   A machine from the Foxboro Rotary Shuttle Company, Foxboro, Mass, which appeared about 1882.

F. Frank, London   Agent or importer of Raymond machines.

Franklin Sewing Machine Company, Birmingham, England   See Royal Franklin.

Franklin   It is believed this machine was produced only in 1871, built by the Franklin Sewing Machine Company, Mason Village, New Hampshire.

Free   The Free Sewing Machine Company, Rockford, Illinois, was established in 1898 and still exists. It is believed that they also produced a machine under the name Knickerbocker. It is not known if this had any connection with the Knickerbocker Sewing Machine Company, which built the Little Worker machine.

French, C. A., Boston, Mass   Maker of the Novelty machine from 1869.

Frister & Rossmann, Berlin   Makers of sewing machines from about 1870. Machines carrying this name are in existence which have a close resemblance to Willcox & Gibbs and Wheeler & Wilson models (see page 89), but most that have survived are of the New Family type. In England Frister & Rossmann machines were imported by:
Hermann Loog Limited, London, from c1883; S. Loewe,

London, c1898–c1901; W. Pierssene, London, c1901–14 (in their catalogue of 1911 Whiteley's of London listed various models priced between £2 16s to £6 6s); O. Quitmann, London, 1920–63.

Between 1925 and 1963 Frister & Rossmann machines were built by Gritzner-Kayser of Karlsruhe-Durlach who also offered machines under their own name. The latter company was taken over by the Pfaff organisation in 1963.

Gardner   Made by C. R. Gardner, Detroit, Michigan, from 1856.

Gardner Sewing Machine Company, Hamilton, Ontario, Canada   Makers of the Canadian, Royal and Royal A machines. The company was established sometime before 1884.

Garfield Sewing Machine Company   An American manufacturer from 1881.

Garvie & Wood   In 1882 a musical sewing machine cover was manufactured in the United States by George D. Garvie and George Wood.

Gem   A machine sold from Symon's Patent (established 1852), George Street, Blackfriars, London. In 1868 the Gem was sold for £4.

General Favorite   Introduced in 1872 as one of the range of machines produced by the Weed Sewing Machine Company, Hartford, Conn.

Geneva Sewing Machine Company   No details available about this American manufacturer. Believed to have produced machines in the 1880s.

Ghul & Harbeck, Hamburg   Makers of the Original Express sewing machine. Production dates not known.

Gibbons, James   With John Fisher, Gibbons was granted a British patent in 1844 for a machine using an eye-pointed needle and a shuttle.

Page 89   Thought to have been built about 1875, this German Frister &
Rossmann double lock-stitch treadle machine bears a striking resemblance
to the American Wheeler & Wilson machines built between 1856 and 1876

Page 90 (above) Hand-painted chain-stitch machine, thought to be built by E.B. of Paris; (below) 1886 patent Moldacot sewing machines. The left-hand one was built in Germany while that on the right is of London origin

Globe   A single-thread chain-stitch built by J. G. Folsom, Winchendon, Mass, between 1865 and 1869.

Globe   Built by James Weir, Soho, London. A surviving instruction booklet carries this explanation: 'in consequence of J.G.W.'s Newly Patented Weir's 55 shilling Sewing Machine, the old pattern 55 shilling Machine is now known and sold as "The Globe Family Sewing Machine" '. The Globe bears a very strong resemblance to the conventional Weir machines (see plate on page 72) but the bobbin holder is single-ended.

Gloria   The Whiteley's (London) catalogue of 1911 lists two machines of this make. One at £1 19s 6d, and a vibrating shuttle model at £2 16s.

Glory   A lock-stitch machine that bears a considerable likeness to Frister & Rossmann New Family models. The trade mark is a ship in full sail.

Goddard, Rice & Company, Worcester, Mass   Makers of Blodgett & Lerow machines in 1849 and 1850.

Godiva   Built in Coventry. Designed by James Starley.

Gold Hibbard   Built by B. S. Hibbard & Company, USA, from 1875.

Gold Medal   A chain-stitch machine built by the Gold Medal Sewing Machine Company, Orange, Mass, between 1863 and 1876. There was also a running-stitch machine of the same name made between 1863 and c1865, but it is not known if this was a product of the same factory.

Goodbody   A *sewing shears* type of machine built by the Goodbody Sewing Machine Company, Bridgeport, Conn, between 1880 and c1890.

Goodes   A machine built by Rex & Rockius, Philadelphia. Production was commenced about 1876 and ended before 1881.

Goodrich   Built by H. B. Goodrich, Chicago, between c1880 and

F   91

c1895. From c1895 until c1920 the machine was made by the Foley & Williams Manufacturing Company.

Goodspeed & Wyman Makers of the Bartlett machine between 1866 and c1870, after which it was produced by the Bartlett Sewing Machine Company, New York, until 1872.

Gordon & Gotch, 15 St Bride Street, London Marketed the American Domestic (Little Domestic) machine, priced at £4 4s in the 1880s.

Gove & Howard An American manufacturer who is thought to have built sewing machines from 1855.

Grant Brothers & Company, Philadelphia Makers of a chain-stitch machine incorporating Charles Raymond's patent of 1861 between the years 1867 and c1870. The price of $18 was expensive compared with other chain-stitch machines (see Fig 17).

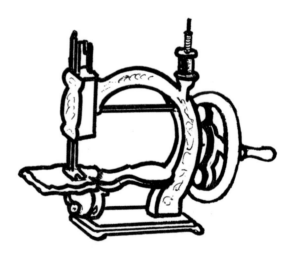

Fig 17 The 1867 Grant sewing machine built under the Charles Raymond 1861 US patent for chain-stitch mechanism

Grasshopper The unofficial *works* name given to the Singer Family machine introduced in 1858.

Graves, J. G., Limited, Sheffield   Agent or importer of Vibra machines.

Greenman & True   A lock-stitch machine based on S. H. Roper's US patent of 1857. Jared F. Greenman and Cyrus B. True produced the machine between 1859 and 1861. At the Massachusetts Charitable Mechanics Exhibition of 1860 the machine was referred to as the Morse & True.

Green Mountain   An American sewing machine built about 1860.

Greenough, John J.   In 1842 Greenough was granted the first American patent specifically applied to a sewing machine.

Greenwood & Company, Miles, Cincinnati, Ohio   Built machines from c1861.

Gresham & Craven, Manchester   Granted patent in March 1867. Makers of the Gresham, Reversable Gresham, and Improved Gresham machines. These were being marketed in 1873, the Gresham priced at £6 4s.

Griffiths, G., Birmingham, England   Listed as sewing machine manufacturer 1864–5.

Griswold Variety   Built by L. Griswold, New York, between c1886 and c1890.

Gritzner-Kayser, Karlsruhe-Durlach, Germany   Built Frister & Rossmann machines between 1925 and 1963, when the company was absorbed by the Pfaff organisation. Machines were also built under the company's name.

Grout & White, Orange, Mass   The partnership of William Grout and Thomas H. White, building New England machines for a short period after 1862.

Grover & Baker   Built by the Grover & Baker Sewing Machine Company, Boston, Mass, between 1851 and 1875. This was the partnership of two Boston tailors, William C. Grover and William E. Baker. The company was succeeded by the Union Special Machine Company.

Guelph   The name of a machine marketed in England in 1873. Probably built by Charles Raymond at Guelph, Ontario, Canada. In the 1870s S. Smith & Co, Soho Bazaar, London, were offering the Guelph machine at £3.

Gutman   An American make about which no information is available.

Haid & Neu, Karlsruhe, Germany   Design similar to other European low-handled machines such as those made by Dietrich & Winselmann.

Hancock   An American make based on the patent of Henry J. Hancock granted in 1867. Production was started in 1868 and ceased before 1881. The early models of this chain-stitch machine used a tambour-type needle. Later models had an eye-pointed needle.

Hancock & Bennett   An American make. No information available.

Harewood, Charles & William, Birmingham, England   Production dates 1860–72.

Harris, Daniel   US inventor of the Boudoir machine covered by patents issued in 1857 and 1858.

Harris & Company Limited, W. J., London   Factors of Brunswick-built machines. A Harris No 3 machine was marketed about 1900.

Harris & Judson   Patent registered in 1871 upon which was based the Challenge machine built by the Imperial Sewing Machine Company, Soho, Birmingham, England. No production dates available.

Harris Patent Sewing Machine   Alternative name for the Boudoir.

Hartford   One of the range of sewing machines built by the Weed Sewing Machine Company, Hartford, Conn. This machine was introduced in 1881 and production continued until c1900.

Heberling Running Stitch   Produced in the USA by John Heberling between 1878 and c1885.

Helpmate   Built by C. W. Williams Manufacturing Company, Montreal, Canada. In the early period of production the machine was known as the New Williams. Manufacture started before 1880 and ended pre-1890.

Henderson   No particulars known about this American make.

Henderson, James   In company with Thomas Stone, Henderson was issued with a French patent in 1804 covering a stitching device.

Hendrick, Joseph   Granted US patent under which Sewing Shears were made by Nettleton & Raymond, Bristol, Conn, from about 1859.

Hensel, George, New York   Granted US patent in 1859.

Herron, Abial C.   Granted US patent in 1857. A chain-stitch machine to this patent was built, but the manufacturer and production dates are not known.

Heyer's Pocket Sewing Machine   A simple stitching appliance patented in America in 1863. It is not known how long production lasted.

Hibbard, B. S.   American manufacturer who produced the Gold Hibbard from 1875.

Highbury Vibrating Shuttle   An American make. No details available.

Highby   Built by the Highby Sewing Machine Company, Brattleboro, Vermont, from about 1882. The machine was later known as the Acme, and was still in production in 1886.

Hill, USA   No information available.

Home and **Home Shuttle**   Built by Johnson, Clark & Company, Orange, Mass, from 1869 and was being marketed after 1876 The New Home Sewing Machine Company, of Orange, was founded in 1876 and still exists, affiliated with the Free Sewing Machine Company, Chicago, from 1928.

Homestead   An American make dating from about 1881.

Hood, Batelle & Company   American manufacturers in 1854.

Hook, Albert H.   Inventor of a small and simple sewing machine. Granted US patent in 1858. The machine was not a commercial success.

Horse   James Perry was granted a US patent in 1858 covering machine designed in the shape of a horse (see page 71).

Household   Built by the Providence Tool Company, Providence, RI, USA, between 1880 and c1884. From about 1885 until 1906 the machine was produced by the Household Sewing Machine Company.

Howard & Davis, Boston, Mass   Makers of the Robinson and Robinson & Roper machines from 1855. Production ceased before 1860.

Howe   The Howe Sewing Machine Company, New York, was established by Amasa B. Howe in 1854, making machines under licence to his brother Elias, who had patented the lock-stitch machine in 1846. Elias set up the Howe Machine Company (omitting the world Sewing) at Bridgeport, Conn. After the death of Elias in 1867, the Bridgeport concern was run by his sons-in-law, the Stockwell Brothers. In about 1873, the Howe Sewing Machine Company (Amasa's company) was sold to the Stockwell Brothers, who continued to manufacture under the name, Howe Machine Company, until 1886. The Howe company had a depot at 160 North Street, Brighton, Sussex—this address appeared in the 1883 Directory.

Howe's Improved Patent   J. B. Nichols was one of Elias Howe's first licensees and in 1853, working in the partnership of Nichols & Bliss, built 28 machines at Boston, Mass. The following year he continued to manufacture as J. B. Nichols & Company. Later in the same year, 1854, the concern became Nichols, Leavitt & Company. In 1855 the machine was sold under the name Leavitt, the company dropping the Nichols part of the name in 1857.

Howland, Charles W.   Maker in Wilmington, USA, about 1860.

N. Hunt   The name of a machine based on the patents of Christopher Hodgkins dated 1852, and built by Nehemiah Hunt & Company, Boston, in 1853. In 1856 the company became Hunt & Webster and, in 1858, Ladd & Webster. In each case the machines made in that period carried the names of the appropriate partners.

Hunt, Walter, New York   The inventor of a lock-stitch machine between 1832 and 1834. The invention was not patented.

Hurtu   French manufacturers of sewing machines who, in about 1885, turned their attention to motor engineering.

Husqvana   The Husqvana Company of Sweden has its origins as a manufacturer of firearms in 1689. The production of sewing machines began in 1872. Makers of the Viking sewing machine.

Ideal   A machine covered by British patent 30,264, involving the walking presser foot.

Imperial Sewing Machine Company, Soho, Birmingham, England Makers of the Challenge machine, using the Harris & Judson patent of 1871. An Imperial model was being offered in the 1870s by S. Smith & Company, Soho Bazaar, London, at £6 16s 6d. Production dates 1876–7.

Improved Buckeye   See Buckeye.

Improved Common Sense   Made in the USA about 1870. The design so closely resembles the New England (USA) and the Weir (England) machines that it is hard to believe there were no connections between those concerned with the three productions. New England machines were made from c1859, while the Weir, said to be based on the 1859 patent of Frederick W. Parker, appeared about 1872.

Improved Gresham   See Gresham & Craven.

Independent Noiseless   Built by the Independent Sewing Machine Company, Binghampton, New York, from 1873. It is not known when production ceased.

Ismak   A British make of machine. Production dates and other details unknown.

J.S. & S.   No particulars known.

Jenks   No information available about this American machine.

Jenny June   Built by the June Manufacturing Company, Chicago, between 1881 and 1890. Sometime in this period the company moved to Belvidere, Illinois.

Jenny Lind   Original name under which Singer's first machine was sold. This was soon changed to Singer's Perpendicular Action Sewing Machine.

Jewel   Built by the Jewel Manufacturing Company, Toledo, Ohio, from 1884. Production ceased sometime after 1886.

Johnson   A machine of ornate design built by Emery, Houghton & Company, Boston, Mass, from 1856 until after 1865.

Johnson, Clark & Company, Orange, Mass   Makers of the Home (1869–c1876), National (from 1874) and Union (from 1876).

Johnson, Joseph B.   In association with Charles Morey, Johnson was granted a US patent in 1849 covering a sewing machine.

Johnson, William   Patentee of machines built by J. H. Lester of Brooklyn, from about 1856.

Jones & Lee   Makers of the Watson machine from 1850 to 1853, when production was continued by Watson & Wooster, Bristol, Conn.

Jones, Solomon   Granted US patent for electro-motor drive in 1871.

Jones   William Jones, Guide Bridge, Audenshaw, Lancashire, built sewing machines under licence, of both Howe and Wilson designs from about 1859. The patent covering Jones's own design was granted in 1869. The company exists to this day, since 1968 as part of the Brother Industries.

Judkins   A machine built by the English inventor Charles T. Judkins was shown at The Great Exhibition of 1851. The Judkins, which also carried the name 'Elastic Chain Stitch', was marketed in 1867 by Wonder, 4 Ludgate Street, London. Production dates unknown (see Fig 4).

June Manufacturing Company, Chicago   Later of Belvidere, Illinois. Makers of the Jenny June (1881–90). In 1890 there was an amalgamation of the June and the Eldridge companies which resulted in the National Sewing Machine Company, Belvidere, Illinois. Production continued until 1953.

Junker & Ruh, Karlsruhe, Baden, Germany   Makers of the SD 28 leather stitcher and other machines. No production dates available.

Kay & Company, Baden   Makers of the Paragon lock-stitch machine. Production period unknown.

Kayser   See Frister & Rossmann.

Kerry A marque of German-produced machine. Production dates unknown.

Ketchum, Stephen C. Inventor whose US patent of 1863 was used on a number of machines.

Keystone Built by the Keystone Sewing Machine Company, USA. The production period was pre-1872 until c1874. There was a Keystone typewriter built from about 1899 but it is unlikely that there was any connection.

Kildare Listed in the London store Whiteley's catalogue of 1911. Treadle and table models were available at £4 17s 6d and £3 3s.

Kimbull & Morton Limited, Glasgow A. Kimbull was listed in the Glasgow Post Office Directory for the first time in 1859 as an agent for Singer. In 1868 the name of Kimbull & Morton Limited appears as manufacturers of sewing machines, production continuing until 1955. At some time Kimbull & Morton built a treadle machine with the head cast in the shape of a lion. The company also made machines for sail-making, sack-making and tarpaulin work, and by c1910, cycles and wringers (see Fig 8).

Knickerbocker Probably made by the Free Sewing Machine Company, Rockford, Illinois. Production dates unknown.

Knickerbocker Machine Company, New York Maker of the Little Worker machine. Patent dates of 1911 and 1912 are carried.

Knowles, John, Monkton, Vermont Said to have built a sewing machine in 1818 or 1819.

Krems, Balthasar, Mayen, Germany Inventor of a chain-stitch machine in 1810.

Lacy & Company, B. W., Philadelphia Makers of the McLean & Hooper machine between c1869 and c1873. After 1873 the Centennial Sewing Machine Company, Philadelphia, built the Centennial machine based on the McLean patents. Production ceased in 1876.

Ladd & Webster, Boston, Mass   See N. Hunt.

Ladies' Companion   Built in Boston, Mass, under the patents of Samuel F. Pratt. Production began in 1857 as the Pratt's Patent machine. In 1859 the machine was marketed as the Ladies Companion, a decorative pedestal treadle machine.

Lady   A remarkable machine of considerable ornamentation, made under the 1849 patent of Isaac F. Baker. The head of the machine was cast to depict Cora Munro, a character from James Fenimore Cooper's book *The Last of the Mohicans*. A second design patented by Baker depicted Major Heyward, another character from the book. George Hensel of New York and Sidney Parker of Sing Sing, NY, were also involved in the patent applications. Only two examples are known to survive from 1859 when they were produced.

The Lady's   A chain-stitch machine marketed by James Weir, London. In 1867 the price was £4. In the 1870s, S. Smith & Company, Soho Bazaar, London, were offering a machine called The Lady at £2 15s. This may have been the same make.

La Favorite   No information available on this American machine.

Lamb, George, Birmingham, England   Listed as sewing machine manufacturer in 1864.

Landfear's Patent   A single-thread chain-stitch machine of decorative design built by Parkers, Snow, Brooks & Company, West Meridan, Conn, from 1857. This concern is possibly related to the Charles Parker Company of Meridan, who built a Parker machine in the 1860s.

Langdon   American inventor Leander W. Langdon's machine was made from 1856. Leander's patent was used on the Florence machine built at Florence, Mass, between 1860 and c1878.

Lansom, Goodnow & Yale, Windsor, Vermont Makers of the Clark's Revolving Looper machine from 1859 to 1861. This concern succeeded the Vermont Arms Company.

E. T. Lathbury's Patent Also known as the Buell. Built by A. B. Buell, Westmoreland, NY, from about 1860.

Lathrop Built by the Lathrop Combination Sewing Machine Company in the USA from 1873, under the Lebbeus W. Lathrop patents of 1869, 1870 and 1873. Production ceased before 1881. Using two threads the machine was capable of lock-stitch, chain-stitch, and *combined lock- and chain-stitch*.

Lead Marque of a toy machine, similar in appearance to the Singer toy of the early twentieth century. Country of origin and production dates unknown. Until recent years an unmarked toy machine, bearing no maker's name, has been marketed in several countries.

Leader Built by the Leader Sewing Machine Company, Springfield, Mass, from 1882. It is not known when production ceased.

Learned No particulars available about this American marque.

Leavitt The name given to the Howe's Improved Patent machine from 1855. The manufacturer in Boston, Mass, was known as Nichols, Leavitt & Company from 1855 to 1857; Leavitt & Company from 1857 to c1865; Leavitt Sewing Machine Company from c1865 to 1870.

E. E. Lee & Company, New York First manufacturers of A. B. Wilson's machine in 1850.

Leggett No particulars available about this American make.

Leigh (or Leica) & Crawford, 32–3 Brooke Street, Holborn, London Importer of German-built machines.

Lerow, John A. Partner of Sherburne C. Blodgett, whose first sewing machine US patent was issued in 1849. For list of manufacturers see Blodgett & Lerow.

Leslie Revolving Shuttle   Built by the Leslie Sewing Machine Company, Cleveland, Ohio, from 1881. It is not known when production ceased.

Lester   A lock-stitch machine built by J. H. Lester, Brooklyn, NY, between c1858 and 1860. In the latter year the concern was known as the Lester Manufacturing Company, Richmond, Virginia, when it was combined with the Old Dominion Sewing Machine Company. In 1860 and 1861 the machine was made by the Union Sewing Machine Company, Richmond, Virginia, when the company amalgamated with George B. Sloat & Company, makers of the Elliptic machine (see Fig 18).

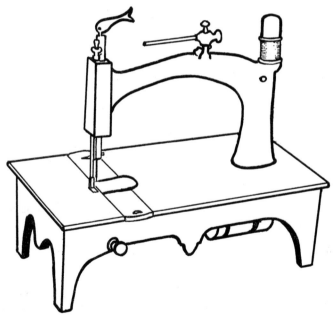

Fig 18   c1858 Lester sewing machine. The American Civil War brought production of the Lester to a halt, then the manufacturing company, called at that time the Union Sewing Machine Company, turned to the making of weapons

Little Domestic   Alternative name given to the American Domestic machine marketed by Gordon & Gotch, London, in the 1880s.

Little Gem   An American machine based on the 1862 patent of Aaron Palmer, inventor of the Fairy machine. Production ceased about 1870.

Little Giant   Built by the Domestic Sewing Machine Company, Norwalk, Ohio, from c1882. Final production date not known.

Little Howe, London   No information available, other than a report of a machine bearing this name having been seen.

Little Monitor   Built by G. L. Du Laney, Brooklyn, NY, from c1866 until after 1875. This machine should not be confused with the Monitor, which was built by Shaw & Clark.

Little Treasure   Built by O. Robinson & Company, Champion Works, Kettering, England. Production dates not known.

Little Wanzer   See Wanzer.

Little Wonder   Built by the New Home Sewing Machine Company, Orange, Mass. This company commenced production in 1876 but it is not known when the Little Wonder was introduced. In 1923 the makers became affiliated with the Free Sewing Machine Company, Rockford, Illinois, a company that still exists. A Little Wonder sewing machine was built by the Slater Sewing Machine Company, Birmingham, England, between 1860–72.

Little Worker   Built by the Knickerbocker Machine Company, New York. Production dates not known.

Loewe, S., 49 Fore Street, London   Importer of Frister & Rossmann machines between c1898 and c1901.

London Sewing Machine   A reference was made in 1849 by the *Scientific American* magazine. This was presumably the machine patented by Barthelemy Thimonnier and Jean Marie Magnin in England on 8 February 1848.

Loog, Hermann, 128 London Wall, London   Importer of Frister

& Rossmann machines from about 1883. The franchise was acquired by S. Loewe c1898 but it is not known if Loog continued to import the machines after this date.

Love Built by the Love Manufacturing Company, Pittsburgh, in 1885. The production was short-lived and disappeared soon after 1886.

Lye, Henry Granted US patent in 1826 for a machine to stitch leather. No description has been found.

Lyon Built by the Lyon Sewing Machine Company in the USA in the years 1879 and 1880.

McArthur & Company, USA No particulars available.

Macauley Built by Thomas A. Macauley Manufacturing Company, New York. It was being sold in 1879 but no production dates are available.

McCardie, USA No particulars available.

McCoy, USA No particulars available.

Mack & Company, William A., Norwalk, Ohio With N. S. Perkins, Mack built the Domestic machine from 1864. In 1869 the company's name was changed to the Domestic Sewing Machine Company. There was an American marque of Mack which was probably also a product of this company. In 1924 William A. Mack & Company was bought by the White Sewing Machine Company, Cleveland, Ohio, and still exists as a subsidiary of that company.

McKay Built by the McKay Sewing Machine Association, USA, between 1870 and 1876.

McKay, Gordon Inventor of a leather stitcher.

McLean & Hooper Built by B. W. Lacy & Company, Philadelphia, from c1869 until c1873. The Centennial, a similar machine, was built by the Centennial Sewing Machine Company, Philadelphia, between 1873 and 1876.

Madersperger, Josef, Vienna, Austria   Inventor of a sewing machine c1816.

Magnin, Jean Marie   Associate of Barthelemy Thimonnier.

Manhattan   Built by the Manhattan Sewing Machine Company, USA, from c1868 until c1880.

Manufacturer's Favorite   One of a range of machines built by the Weed Sewing Machine Company, Hartford, Conn. This machine was introduced in 1868.

Mathies, Robert   Inventor of a leather stitcher patented in 1862.

Maxfield (possibly Mayfield)   Built at Birmingham, England, by Maxfield & Company. Machines carry patent date 1870. Production dates 1876–7.

Mayfield & Company, Agenoria Works, Birmingham, England   Also known as the Franklin Sewing Machine Company and makers of the Agenoria machine.

Medallion   No particulars available about this American make.

Meyers   Built by J. M. Meyers, in the USA, from 1859, until an unknown date.

Miller's Patent   No particulars known about this American make.

Moldacot   A pocket lock-stitch sewing machine patented by S. A. Rosenthal, Berlin, in 1885. It was built in both Germany and in England from 1886 or 1887. In London it was marketed by the Moldacot Pocket Sewing Machine Company.

Monarch   Marketed by Smith & Company, 50 Edgware Road, and Charles Street, Soho, London. Production dates not known.

Monitor   Built by Shaw & Clark Sewing Machine Company, Biddeford, Maine, USA, between 1860 and 1864. Not to be confused with the Little Monitor made later by G. L. Du Laney, Brooklyn. The Monitor used a top-feed *walking* presser foot.

Monopoly   No particulars available about this American machine.

Page 107   Complexity of Singer attachments in the early twentieth century

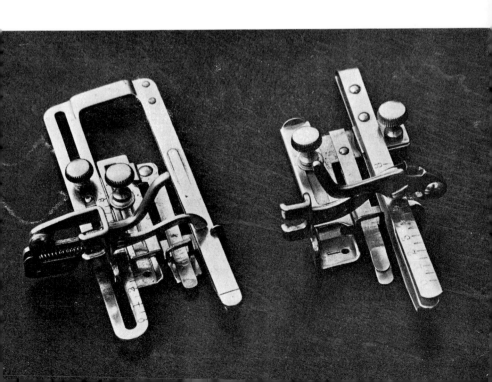

Page 108 The author (left) with fellow collector B. Figgett, at an outdoor event attended by the Veteran Machine Register

Moore Built by the Moore Sewing Machine Company, USA, from c1860.

Moore, W. B., Dublin and Cork There are examples of Weir machines with separate cast-iron bases carrying this name.

Moreau No particulars available about this American make.

Morey & Johnson Charles Morey and Joseph S. Johnson were granted a US patent in 1849. The machine was built by Safford & Williams, Boston, Mass, from 1849 until c1851.

Morrison Built by Morrison, Wilkinson & Company, Hartford, Conn, from 1881.

Morrison & Company, James, USA Marketed a fanning attachment for sewing machines in the 1870s.

Morse & True In 1860 the machine known as the Greenman & True was referred to as the Morse & True. No further information is available. See also Greenman & True.

Mower No information available about this American marque which appeared c1863.

Müller A toy machine built in Germany. No production dates known.

Na Del Qualitat A German-built machine. A model known as the 339 bears a resemblance to Frister & Rossmann machines.

National Built by Johnson, Clark & Company, Orange, Mass, from 1874 until an unknown date.

National Built by the National Sewing Machine Company, Belvidere, Illinois, from 1890 until 1953. This concern was an amalgamation of the June Manufacturing Company and the Eldridge Sewing Machine Company, both of Chicago. The machine was also sold under names of distributors.

National Sewing Machine Company, London Marketed the Boston Star machine.

Nauman (Naumann?)   A German machine of the New Family type. Production dates unknown. Possibly a product of Seidel & Naumann, Dresden.

Nelson   Built by the New Home Sewing Machine Company, Rockford, Illinois. The company was established in 1876 but no production dates for the machine are known.

Nelson   Probably one of a range of machines built by Adam Opel.

Ne Plus Ultra   A chain-stitch machine built by the O. L. Reynolds Manufacturing Company, Dover, New Hampshire, from 1857 until an unknown date in the 1860s.

Nettleton & Raymond, Bristol, Conn, and later (1858), Brattleboro, Vermont. The partnership of Willford H. Nettleton and Charles Raymond, who commenced manufacture about 1857. The company also produced Sewing Shears, the patent of J. E. Hendrick. Later the New England (Raymond's invention) was produced by this concern. See also Raymond.

New American   The name given to the American Buttonhole, Overseaming and Sewing Machine from c1874 until c1886. Marketed in London by Newton Wilson, 144 High Holborn.

New Boston   The name given to the Boston machine sometime during the production period, 1880 to c1886. Built by J. F. Paul & Company, Boston, Mass, who at sometime changed their name to the Boston Sewing Machine Company.

New Buckeye   At first known as the Buckeye and Improved Buckeye. Built between c1867 and c1876 by the W. G. Wilson Sewing Machine Company, Cleveland, Ohio.

New Cannaan   Nothing known about this American make.

New Dauntless   At first known as the Dauntless and produced by the Dauntless Manufacturing Company, Norwalk, Ohio, from 1877 until after 1882. The company also made the Queen machine.

New Dominion   No information available. There was a machine known as the Old Dominion and built by the Old Dominion Sewing Machine Company, Richmond, Virginia, between c1858 and 1860. There is no evidence of a connection between the *Old* and *New* Dominions.

New England   A machine very similar to the Improved Common Sense (USA) and the Weir (England) machines. The New England, the invention of Charles Raymond, was produced by him between c1859 and 1866. It was also made by Grout & White, Orange, Mass (1862–3); William Grout, Winchendon, Mass (from 1863); J. G. Folsom, also of Winchendon (in 1865 only).

Newell   An American machine built from 1881. No further details.

New Fairbanks   Built by J. H. Drew & Company between 1878 and 1880, and from 1880 up to an unknown date by Thomas M. Cochrane Company, Belleville, Illinois.

New Home   Built by the New Home Sewing Machine Company, Orange, Mass, from 1876 until an unknown year. The company also built the Nelson and Little Wonder machines. In 1928 there was an amalgamation between the New Home and the Free Sewing Machine Companies. The concern still exists under the latter name.

New Stewart   Built by the Stewart Manufacturing Company between 1880 and c1883. Previously, between 1874 and 1880, the machine was known as the Stewart and made by Henry Stewart & Company, New York.

Newton, Edward   With Thomas Archbold, Newton patented a machine for ornamenting the backs of gloves in 1841.

Newton Wilson   Newton Wilson & Company, 144 High Holborn, London, with a factory in Birmingham, were makers of machines between c1862 and c1894. In 1862 Wilson displayed a Grover & Baker machine at the International Exhibition, South Kensington, London. In 1867 the company was marketing the Cleopatra, Queen Mab, Dorcas and American Buttonhole, Overseaming and Sewing Machine. The *Kelly's Directory* of 1879 described Newton Wilson as 'Patentees and manufacturers of sewing machines, bicycles, washing machines and mangles, and of horse-grooming, horse-clipping and sheep-shearing machines'. From 1885 the address was listed as Southampton Row and Hilldrop Road, Camden Town. In 1874 Wilson discovered the patent specification of the sewing machine invented by Thomas Saint in 1790 (see pages 17 and 25).

New York   A make of machine built in New York, probably only in the year 1855.

New York Shuttle   Built by the New York Sewing Machine Company, NY, from before 1880. In 1882 the company's name was changed to the Demorest Manufacturing Company.

Niagra   Nothing known about this American make.

Nichols & Company, J. B.   Makers of machines to the Howe patent during 1854 under this name. See also Howe's Improved Patent for variations in the company's style.

Noble   Built by the Noble Sewing Machine Company, Erie, Pa. Production was started before 1881 and was carried on until after 1886.

Novelty   Built by C. A. French, Boston, Mass, from 1869 to an unknown year. There was another American machine sold under the name, Ten Dollar Novelty, produced about 1870, but it is not known if there is a connection with C. A. French.

Old Dominion   Built by the Old Dominion Sewing Machine Company, Richmond, Virginia, between c1858 and 1860. In 1860 the company amalgamated with the Lester Manufacturing Company.

Opel   See Adam Opel.

Original Brunonia   A machine similar to a model marketed by the Atlas Machine Company, London. One example carries the name of an agent: B. Segrestani, Alexandrie, Egypte (sic).

Original Express   Made by Ghul & Harbeck, Hamburg, Germany. Production dates not known.

Orphean, USA   No particulars available.

Palmer, Aaron   Granted US patents in 1862 under which the Fairy and Little Gem machines were made.

Paragon   Lock-stitch machine built by Kay & Company, Baden. Production dates not known.

Pardox   An American machine built from c1865. No other particulars available.

Parham   Built by the Parham Sewing Machine Company, Philadelphia, from c1869 until c1871.

Parker   Built by Charles Parker, Meridan, Conn, before 1860 until after 1865. Later the maker was known as the Parker Sewing Machine Company. There is a possibility of a relationship with Parkers, Snow, Brooks & Company, West Meridan, Conn, who made the Landfear's Patent machine from 1857.

Parker, Samuel J.   Granted patent under which the American Magnetic machine was made in 1854.

Parker, Sidney, New York   Granted US patent for a sewing machine in 1859.

Parkers, Snow, Brooks & Company, West Meridan, Conn. Makers of the Landfear's Patent machine from 1857.

Paul & Company, J. F., Boston, Mass   Makers of the Boston machine from 1880. The name was changed to the Boston Sewing Machine Company, who produced the New Boston machine. Production dates are not known but the New Boston was being sold in 1886.

Pearl   Built by a company called Bennett in the USA from c1859.

There was a manufacturer by the name of Bennett in Chicago who built the Boudoir machine, but there is no evidence of any connections.

Peerless also **Sarti's Peerless**   No information available.

Penelope   A lock-stitch machine marketed in 1867 by Newton Wilson, London, priced at £5 5s.

People's Sewing Machine   Built by Slater & Company, 133 Tennant Street, Birmingham, England. No production dates known.

Perkins, N. S.   See Domestic.

Perkins & Marshall, Northamptonshire, England. Referred to as sewing machine manufacturers in the 1869 Post Office Directory.

Perry, James   American inventor and patentee in 1858 of the unusual horse-shaped sewing machine.

Pfaff   In 1963 the Pfaff organisation absorbed the company of Gritzner-Kayser of Karlsruhe-Durlach, who had been making Frister & Rossmann machines since 1925.

Phelps, O., Boston, Mass   Maker of the Blodgett & Lerow machine in 1849.

Philadelphia   Built by the Philadelphia Sewing Machine Company between c1872 and c1881.

Pierssene, W., London   Importer of Frister & Rossmann machines between c1901 and 1914.

Porter, L. & A.   American patentees (1869 and 1870) of the Atlantic machine built in the 1870s.

Post Combination   Built by the Post Combination Sewing Machine Company, Washington, DC. Production started prior to 1885 but was discontinued soon after 1886.

Potter, Orlando B.   President of the Grover & Baker Company and founder of the Sewing Machine Combination in 1856.

Pratt's Patent Built in Boston, Mass, under patents of Samuel F. Pratt. Production was started in 1857. The machine was renamed the Ladies' Companion in 1859.

Pride-of-the-West, USA No particulars available.

Princess Built in Nuremburg, Germany. A children's chain-stitch machine cast in the shape of a woman's figure sitting at a sewing table (see Fig 1). Production dates not known.

Princess Built by the Decker Manufacturing Company, Detroit, Michigan, for an unknown period before 1881.

Princess Beatrice Origin not known. In the 1870s, S. Smith & Company, Soho Bazaar, London, were offering this machine at £2 10s.

Princess of Wales A machine listed by S. Smith & Company, Soho Bazaar, London, priced at £4 4s. This was probably the machine made by William Jones of Guide Bridge, Lancashire, which carried the slogan 'As supplied to HRH the Princess of Wales'. Or one with similar inscription by Newton Wilson.

Providence Tool Company, Providence, Rhode Island, USA Makers of the Household machine between 1880 and c1884 after which year it was built by the Household Sewing Machine Company.

Puritan An American leather stitching machine. Production dates and manufacturer not known.

Quaker City Built by the Quaker City Sewing Machine Company, Philadelphia, from 1859 until c1861. The price of the treadle model was $150. The machine was based on the 1858 patents of William P. Uhlinger.

Queen Built by the Dauntless Manufacturing Company, Norwalk, Ohio, from c1881 for an unrecorded period. The company also built the Dauntless and New Dauntless machines.

Queen Mab A machine marketed by Newton Wilson, London.

In 1867 machines were priced at £3 3s and £4 4s. In the 1870s, S. Smith & Company, Soho Bazaar, London, were offering Queen Mab machines at £2 15s.

Querida A make probably built in Germany. It bears a similarity to the Haid & Neu machine. Production dates not known.

Quitmann, O., London Importer of Frister & Rossmann machines from 1920 until 1963. Since that date the company has imported Japanese machines and marketed them under the Frister & Rossmann label.

Raymond Charles Raymond was the inventor of the New England machine produced by several US manufacturers between c1859 and 1866. A Raymond machine with the patent date 1872 was built by Charles Raymond at Guelph, Ontario, Canada, between c1873 and after 1884. A surviving example of this marque carries the name of the agent as Watts of Plymouth, England. A New England style machine carrying the name Raymond as well as F. Frank, London, was sold at a Christie's sale in 1973 (see Fig 19).

Regina A machine, probably of German make, very similar in design to Frister & Rossmann and other New Family styles.

Remington Empire Built between 1870 and 1872 by the Remington Empire Sewing Machine Company. At some moment in production the word Empire was dropped from the name and manufacture was undertaken by E. Remington, Philadelphia, between 1873 and c1894. Prior to the Remington production the machine was built between c1860 and 1870 by the Empire Company, Boston, Mass, and sold as the Empire. Remington also produced other machines including typewriters, agricultural implements and, of course, guns.

Reversible Gresham See Gresham and Craven.

Rex & Rockius, Philadelphia Makers of the Goodes machine between c1876 and sometime before 1881.

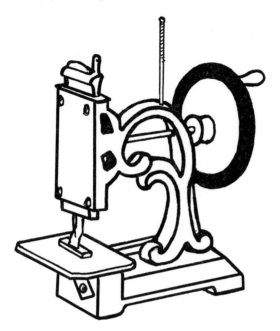

Fig 19 The 1858 patent model of Charles Raymond featuring a hinged presser foot acting as a top-feed. Three years later Raymond was granted a US patent for an improved looper. The date 30 July 1861 is found on all later Raymond machines

Reynolds Manufacturing Company, O. L., Dover, New Hampshire Makers of the Ne Plus Ultra machine from 1857. It is not known when production ceased.

Robertson, T. J. W., New York Inventor of the Cherub and Dolphin machines made by D. W. Clark, Bridgeport, Conn, between 1857 and the early 1860s. It is believed Robertson built sewing machines from 1855.

Robinson Built by F. R. Robinson, Boston, Mass, between 1853 and c1855.

Robinson's Patent Sewing Machine Built by Howard & Davis, Boston, Mass, from 1855. Frederick Robinson's patent was granted in 1850 and a patent of Samuel Roper of 1854 was incorporated in the design. In 1856 additional improvements by Roper were introduced and the Robinson & Roper machine continued in production, ceasing sometime before 1860. The machine was priced at $100.

Robinson & Company, O., Champion Works, Kettering, England Makers of the Little Treasure machine which also carried the Champion trade mark. The machine is marked Robinson's Patent. Years of production 1856–82.

Royal and **Royal A** Built by the Gardner Sewing Machine Company, Hamilton, Ontario, Canada, from about 1884. Some machines may have been named Royal Gardner.

Royal Anchor See Thomas Bradford & Company.

Royal Franklin Built by the Franklin Sewing Machine Company, Soho, Birmingham, England. This factory also made the Agenoria machine. Also known as Mayfield & Company; one surviving example is marked with this name. Production dates 1870–2, according to Birmingham trade directories.

Royal Sewing Machine Company Limited (Shakespeare & Illiston), Small Heath, Birmingham, England Makers of the Shakespeare machine. Production dates 1870–88.

Royal Sewing Machine Company, Springfield, Ohio Makers of the Royal St John machine from c1883 until 1893. Initially the St John machines were built by the St John Sewing Machine Company of Springfield, between 1870 until the company was renamed. The Royal Sewing Machine Company was absorbed in the Free Sewing Machine Company of Chicago in 1898.

Royal St John See Royal Sewing Machine Company, Springfield, Ohio, above.

Ruddick, USA Production started about 1860. No other particulars available.

Rushford In appearance like Singer New Family machines. Origin and production dates not known.

S.D. S.D. 28 was the designation given to a leather stitcher made by Junker & Ruh, Karlsruhe, Baden, Germany. No production dates known.

S.D. & Company, London Marketed the Express machine which was probably of German origin. The machine carried the slogan 'We Move with the Times'. S.D. probably stands for S. Davis who imported the Beaumont machine and it is likely that there was a connection with the Atlas Machine Company, Camden Town.

Safford & Williams, Boston, Mass Makers of the Morey & Johnson machine from 1849 until c1851.

Saint, Thomas, London Patentee of a leather stitcher in 1790. The first recorded invention of a sewing machine.

Sanspareil Built by William Andrews, Birmingham, England, in the 1860s.

Sawstone & Anderson, 78 High Street, Clapham, London Probably agents. An example of this marque bears a resemblance to the New Family type of machine.

Saxonia A lock-stitch machine, presumably built in Germany, marketed by the American Sewing Machine Company, London. No production dates known. Probably made by Gustav Winselmann.

Saxony A lock-stitch machine built by Gustav Winselmann GmbH, Attenburg, Saxony. Production dates not known.

Scates, Tryber & Sweetland Manufacturing Company, Chicago, Illinois Makers of the Chicago Singer machine between 1879 and 1882. In 1882 the company became known as the Chicago Sewing Machine Company.

Seamen & Guiness, USA   No particulars known.

Secor   Built by the Secor Machine Company, Bridgeport, Conn, between 1870 and 1876. The Empress machine was manufactured on order through Jerome B. Secor of Bridgeport from 1877.

Segrestani, B. Alexandrie, Egypte (sic)   Importer or agent for the Original Brunonia machine.

Seidel & Naumann, Dresden, Germany   The English importers' or agents' address was 23 Moor Lane, London, EC2. No production dates known. Seidel & Naumann also built the Ideal typewriter from 1897.

Sellers & Sons, William, Airedale Works, Keighley, Yorkshire Makers of Stitchwell machines. The company was established in 1854 but it is not known when production ceased. Sellers were also makers of knitting machines, wringers and other domestic equipment, baby carriages and coin-operated machines.

Service   No information available other than this was a German-built machine.

Sewing Shears   Made by Nettleton & Raymond, Bristol, Conn, from about 1859. The machine was made under the patent granted to Joseph Hendrick. Some machines could both sew and cut in the same operation.

Sewing Shears   Made by the American Hand Sewing Machine Company, Bridgeport, Conn, from c1884 until c1900.

Shakespeare   Built by Shakespeare & Illiston, The Royal Sewing Machine Company, Birmingham, England. No production dates known. In the 1870s, S. Smith & Company, Soho Bazaar, London, were offering the Shakespeare machine at £4 4s.

Shanks, USA   No particulars known.

Shaw & Clark   The Shaw & Clark Company made machines at Biddeford, Maine, between 1857 and 1866. In 1867 the company moved to Cicopee Falls, Mass, and in 1868 took the name Cicopee Sewing Machine Company, but remained in business only for about one year. The Monitor machine was built by Shaw & Clark between 1860 and 1864, and the company made a variety of running-stitch and chain-stitch machines.

Shepherd, Rothwell & Hughes, Oldham, England Makers of the Eclipse series of sewing machines. These were advertised in 1873 but production dates are not known. The range included Family, Medium, and 'A', 'B' and 'C' models.

Shuttle Anchor A machine marketed by Thomas Bradford & Company, London. This was advertised in 1871 but production dates are not known.

Shuttle Express Marketed by the Howe Sewing Machine Company, 27 Holborn Viaduct, London, EC. The identity of the manufacturer is unknown but could possibly be Ghul & Harbeck, Hamburg, who made the Original Express machine.

Shu—— Express A machine entered in the Veteran Machine Register carries this transfer. The missing letters may have made up the word 'shuttle'. The identity of the maker is unknown but could possibly be Ghul & Harbeck, Hamburg, who made the Original Express machine.

Sigwalt Built by the Sigwalt Sewing Machine Company, Chicago, Illinois, from about 1879. The following year the name Diamond was given to the machine. The year when production ceased is not known.

Simplex No information.

Singer Production started in 1850 as I. M. Singer & Company at Boston, Mass. Up to 1858 the output was confined to heavy machines of the manufacturing type. In 1858 the Family (the Grasshopper or Turtleback as it was known) was introduced— a model that was made until 1861. The Transverse Shuttle— Letter A machine was made between 1859 and 1865, when the

New Family was produced. This continued to be made until 1883, when the Improved Family made its appearance. The name of the company was changed at an early stage to the Singer Manufacturing Company and subsequent moves have taken the factory from Boston, to New York, and to Elizabethport, New Jersey (see pages 35 and 36).

Slater Sewing Machine Company, 133 Tennant Street, Birmingham, England   Makers of the People's Sewing Machine, and Little Wonder sewing machines. Production dates 1860–72.

Sloat & Company, George B., Philadelphia   Makers of the Sloat's Elliptic machine from about 1858. In 1860 the company combined with the Lester Manufacturing Company and the amalgamation became known as the Union Sewing Machine Company, Richmond, Virginia, the machines being sold as Elliptic. Between 1861 and c1867 the machine was built by the Wheeler & Wilson Manufacturing Company, and after 1867 by the Elliptic Sewing Machine Company, New York. The marque was no longer sold in 1880.

Smith & Company, 50 Edgware Road and Charles Street, Soho, London   Marketed the Monarch machine, production dates of which are not known. There was a concern, S. Smith & Company, Soho Bazaar, London, in the 1870s, marketing a considerable range of British- and American-made machines. These two companies were probably related, if not the same.

Smith & Starley, Coventry   Founded in 1869 by Borthwick Smith and James Starley. Makers of the Europa sewing machine.

Smith, Wilson H., Birmingham, Conn   Built machines from c1860. No further particulars known.

So-All   A needle-feed machine about which no particulars are known.

Soeze   Built by Bradbury & Company, Wellington Works, Oldham, England. The company started sewing machine production in 1853.

Sophast Marketed by A. W. Gamage, Holborn, London. Possibly made by Dietrich or Haid & Neu.

Speedwell Origin not known. In the 1870s, S. Smith & Company, Soho Bazaar, London, were offering the machine at £2 10s.

Springfield Built by the Springfield Sewing Machine Company, Springfield, Mass, from 1880.

Squirrel A machine cast in the shape of a squirrel, the subject of an 1857 US patent granted to S. B. Ellithorp and someone by the name of Fox. No examples are known to survive.

Fig 20   No example of this Squirrel sewing machine is known to have survived. The machine was the subject of an American patent granted to S. B. Ellithorp in 1857. The illustration is from the *Sewing Machine News* of 1885

Stackpole, USA   No particulars known.

Standard   A lock-stitch machine built by the Standard Shuttle Sewing Machine Company, New York, from 1874 until c1881. From 1870 the predecessor of this company built a chain-stitch machine. The company's name at that time is unknown.

Standard   Built by the Standard Sewing Machine Company, Cleveland, Ohio, from 1884. The company also made a machine under the name Defiance, which, it is believed, had no connection with the machine of this name built by the Davis Sewing Machine Company, Dayton, Ohio. The Standard company was acquired by Singer and the marque disappeared in about 1930.

Starley, James (1830–81)   Worked for Newton Wilson between 1859 and 1861. He then became foreman at the Coventry Sewing Machine Company, and designed the European sewing machine. In 1869 Starley formed a partnership with Borthwick Smith to build sewing machines. Starley is also a famous name in the field of cycle manufacture.

Steel & Company, James, Cheltenham, England   From c1870 this company had the agency for Howe, Weir, and Newton Wilson machines.

Stewart   Built by Henry Stewart, New York, between 1874 and 1880. From the latter date until c1883 the machine was known as the New Stewart and built by the Stewart Manufacturing Company.

Stitchwell   A series of machines built by William Sellers & Sons, Keighley, Yorkshire. Family, Medium and Hand Stitchwell machines in 1884 were priced between £4 4s and £7 7s.

St John   Built by the St John Sewing Machine Company, Springfield, Ohio, between 1870 and c1883. From the latter date until 1898, the machines were called Royal St John and the maker's name was changed to the Royal Sewing Machine Company.

Stockwell Brothers   The sons-in-law of Elias Howe, who took over the Howe Machine Company, Bridgeport, Conn, in 1867. In 1873 the brothers purchased the Howe Sewing Machine Company which had been founded by Amasa Howe, Elias's elder brother.

Stone, Thomas   With James Henderson, Stone was issued with a French patent in 1804 covering a stitching machine.

Superba 'D' (Syst 182)   A German-made machine. No production dates known. See also Wertheim.

Suprema   A German lock-stitch machine which carried the German eagle as a trade mark. No production dates known.

Surprise, USA   No particulars known.

Sweet, Harry   American patentee in 1853 of a binder attachment.

Swift & Sure   Marketed by Collier & Son, 136 Clapham Road, London. No production dates known.

Swiftsure   Designed by James Starley and built in Coventry. In the 1870s, S. Smith & Company, Soho Bazaar, London, were offering the Swiftsure at £2 2s.

Symon's Patent   A lock-stitch machine sold from George Street, Blackfriars, London. An advertisement of 1868 offers the Gem for £4. The same advertisement states that the company was established in 1852.

Tabitha   Small brass toy machine on a wooden base. Sold in England. Origin not known.

Taggart & Farr, Philadelphia, Pa   Although based on Chester Farr's patent of 1859, this two-thread chain-stitch machine was made in the previous year. Production had ceased by 1881.

Taylor   Origin not known. In the 1870s, S. Smith & Company, Soho Bazaar, London, were offering the Taylor at £4 4s.

Thomas   Built by W. F. Thomas, London. Thomas was the purchaser of Elias Howe's no 3 machine, and patented his own design in 1853. In the 1870s, S. Smith & Company, Soho Bazaar, London, was offering a Thomas chain-stitch machine at £2 15s.

Thomas & Company, Birmingham, England Makers of No 2 and New Domestic sewing machines. Production dates 1862–77.

Thompson Built by the C. F. Thompson Company, USA, in 1871. Production lasted only one year.

Thompson Built by Thomas C. Thompson, Ithaca, New York, about 1854. Thompson was the patentee of the design covering the American Magnetic machines built in 1853 and 1854.

Thurston Manufacturing Company, Marlboro, New Hampshire Maker of the Companion machine from 1882.

Time Utilizer Built by R. M. Wanzer & Company, Hamilton, Ontario, Canada, between 1860 and pre-1890. In 1860 R. M. Wanzer was building sewing machines at Buffalo, New York.

Titan Built by Gustav Winselmann GmbH, Attenburg (Sachsen), Germany. Production dates not known.

Titania One of the range of machines built by Adam Opel, Germany. Production dates not known.

Todd's Champion of England No particulars known. There was a machine Champion built by O. Robinson & Company, Kettering, England, but any suggestion of a connection is speculative.

Tom Hood Origin not known. In the 1870s, S. Smith & Company, Soho Bazaar, London, were offering the Tom Hood at £4 4s.

Triumph No information available.

Troy, USA No particulars known.

Turtleback The name under which Singer's Family machine was advertised.

Uhlinger, William P. Granted US patent in 1858 under which the Quaker City machine was built between 1859 and c1861.

Una   Marketed by the Atlas Machine Company, London. Production dates not known.

Union   Built by Johnson, Clark & Company, Orange, Mass, from 1876.

Union Buttonhole Machine Company   No particulars known.

Union Sewing Machine Company, Richmond, Virginia   The name given to the amalgamation of the Old Dominion Sewing Machine Company and George B. Sloat & Company.

Union Special Machine Company   The company that succeeded the Grover & Baker Sewing Machine Company. The company name was still being used after World War II.

United States Family, USA   No particulars known.

Universal   A chain-stitch machine marketed by the London store Whiteley's in 1911. Price £3 3s.

Universum   A machine of similar appearance to Haid & Neu and other German machines. It was listed in Whiteley's catalogue of 1911. Price £1 15s 6d.

Usha   No particulars known.

Utica, USA   No particulars known.

Varley & Wolfenden, Keighley, Yorkshire   This company was building sewing machines in 1884 but production dates are not known.

Vermont Arms Company, Windsor, Vermont   Built the Windsor single-thread machine between 1856 and 1858. The company was succeeded by Lansom, Goodnow & Yale, who produced the Clark's Revolving Looper machine until 1861.

Vesta   Built by Dietrich in Germany. Production dates not known (see Fig 21).

Vibra   Marked 'Made in S. America'. One example survives that had been sold by J. G. Graves Limited, Sheffield. No other particulars known.

Fig 21   A Vesta treadle sewing machine built by Dietrich in Germany

Vickers   When the supply of Frister & Rossmann machines was curtailed because of World War I, the London importer, W. Pierssene, approached the Vickers company, who were making their post-war production plans, to make a vibrating shuttle machine based on the Frister & Rossmann design. Production was continued until 1934–5.

Victor   Built by Finkle & Lyon Manufacturing Company between 1867 and c1872. The name of the company was then changed to the Victor Sewing Machine Company and production was continued at Middletown, Conn, until about 1890.

Victoria   Sold by the Army & Navy Stores, London. In 1914 the price was £2 19s. Manufacturers and production dates not known.

128

Viking   Built by the Husqvana Company in Sweden.

Vulcan   British make of toy machines.

Wagner, USA   No particulars known.

Wanzer   Built by R. M. Wanzer, Buffalo, NY, in the late 1850s. In 1860 Wanzer set up a factory at Hamilton, Ontario, Canada— the first in that country—making Wanzer and Time Utilizer machines. Production ceased sometime after 1886. R. M. Wanzer purchased the Canada Sewing Machine Company in 1878. The London, England, offices were, in 1867, at 4 Cheapside, and sometime at Great Portland Street. Prices in 1867 ranged from £9 to £15. A machine known as the Little Wanzer was marketed in England in 1873 (see Fig 22).

E. Ward   A British make of an *arm and platform* machine. Production dates not known.

Warde   No particulars known.

Wardwell   Built by the Wardwell Manufacturing Company, St Louis, Mo, from about 1876 until 1900.

Waterbury   Built by the Waterbury Company, Waterbury, Conn, between 1853 and about 1860. Waterbury was famous for inexpensive watch production.

Watson   Built by Jones & Lee between 1850 and c1853 when production was undertaken by Watson & Wooster, Bristol, Conn. The inventor was William C. Watson, whose first recorded patent was issued in 1856, well after the commencement of manufacture. Production ceased about 1860.

Watts & Company, R. I., Plymouth, England   Stockist of a very extensive range of sewing machines between c1864 and 1899. Agent for and possibly importer of Raymond machines.

Weaver, USA   No particulars known.

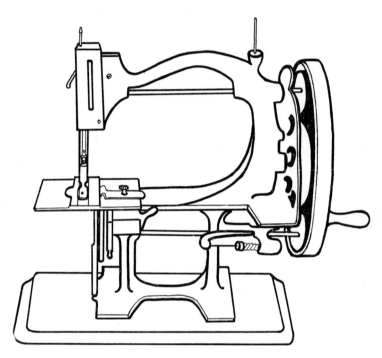

Fig 22 A Wanzer Time Utilizer sewing machine. The last patent date shown is 16 January 1875 and it is also engraved 'Wanzer Sewing Machine Company Limited, Gt Portland St. London'. Illustration based on a drawing by Brian Matthews

Weed Initially made by T. E. Weed & Company from about 1854. Sometime in the late 1850s or early 1860s the company was renamed Whitney & Lyons. In 1865 the company was re-organised and again changed its name, this time to the Weed Sewing Machine Company, which was based at Hartford, Conn. Subsequent models made by the company were: Family Favorite (1867), Manufacturer's Favorite (1868), General Favorite (1872), and Hartford (1881–c1900). Weed machines were being imported into England in 1870. See also Whitney & Lyons.

Weir A machine using a looper which was the subject of a patent issued to Frederick W. Parker, Sheffield, in 1859. The Weir, a small machine on which the reel of thread rides on top of the needle bar, bears a strong resemblance to the New England and Improved Common Sense machines built in the USA. The Weir was produced by James Weir, 2 Carlisle Street, and 42 Hanway Street, Soho, London, from 1872. There is however, in the *Cheltenham Trade Directory* of 1870, an advertisement illustrating a machine which is obviously identical to the Weir. Although all the Weir machines that have come to notice are basically of the same design, it is difficult to find two examples that do not vary in some small way. There were many styles of bases, including a detachable cast-iron base marked 'W. B. Moore, Dublin & Cork'. In the 1870s, S. Smith & Company, Soho Bazaar, London, were offering the Weir machine at £2 15s. Weir also made a sewing machine carrying the name 'Globe'.

Wellington   Built by Bradbury & Company, Wellington Works, Oldham, England, who also produced the Bradbury and Soeze machines. The company started sewing machine manufacture in 1852 and continued until the early years of the twentieth century.

Wells & Haynes, USA   A sewing machine make of c1860.

Wertheim   There is very little information available about this German manufacturer who also made knitting machines. Traces of a Wertheim transfer have been found on a machine which also bears the name Superba 'D' (Syst 182).

Wesson   Built by the Farmer & Gardner Manufacturing Company in 1879 and 1880 when manufacture was undertaken by D. B. Wesson, Springfield, Mass. It is not known when production ceased.

West & Willson   Built by the West & Willson Company (the partnership of H. B. West and H. F. Willson), Elyria, Ohio, from 1858. The machine was made for a very short period. It is thought that single-thread lock-stitch as well as two-thread machines were produced.

Westbournia Sold by the London store Whiteley's in 1911 at £2 10s.

Whalley, Smith & Paget, Parker Street Works, Keighley, Yorkshire   This company was building sewing machines in 1884, but it is not known when production was started or when it ceased.

Wheeler & Wilson   The products of the partnership between Nathaniel Wheeler and Allen B. Wilson. Wilson started work on his first sewing machine in 1847. In 1851, and 1852 his design was used for machines produced by E. E. Lee & Company, New York. The association with Wheeler started in 1851 and the A. B. Wilson's Patent Seaming Lathe was built between that year and 1856 by the Wheeler, Wilson Company, Watertown, New York. In 1856 the company moved to Bridgeport, Conn, and was renamed the Wheeler & Wilson Manufacturing Company, becoming the largest maker of sewing machines in the 1850s and 1860s. From 1905 until 1907 Wheeler & Wilson machines were built by the Singer Company, Bridgeport, Conn. Wheeler & Wilson built the Elliptic machine between 1861 and c1867.
The Wheeler & Wilson No 8 model was introduced in 1876.
The London offices of Wheeler & Wilson were, in 1867, at 43 St Pauls Churchyard and 139 Cheapside, machines selling at prices from £9 to £15.
An Improved Wheeler & Wilson machine was advertised in London under the name Adjustable Belgravia, with a patent date shown as 1868. The address from where this machine was sold was 20 High Holborn.
Another, or possibly the same, Improved Wheeler & Wilson was produced by the Britannia Manufacturing Company, Colchester, England.

Whight & Mann or White & Mann, 143 Holborn Bars, London   Two spellings of the same name have been found. In 1868 this company was marketing the Alberta and Excelsior machines.

White   Built by the White Sewing Machine Company, Cleveland,

Ohio, from 1876. The company is still in existence. Thomas H. White, the inventor, had been engaged in the design and construction of sewing machines for many years before the foundation of this company. He had been associated with the Brattleboro in 1853, and with the New England in 1862–3. Between 1866 and 1876 White was making machines for sale under special trade names through sales organisations. In 1924 the White company acquired the Domestic Sewing Machine Company, makers of the Domestic and Little Giant machines (see Fig 23).

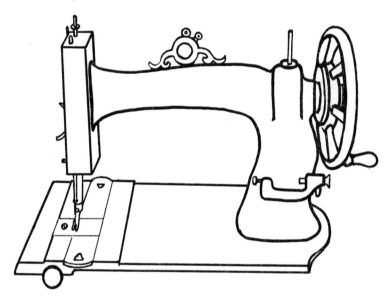

Fig 23   A White sewing machine built between 1876 and 1879

Whitehill   Built by the Whitehill Manufacturing Company, Milwaukee, Wisconsin, from about 1875 and 1886.

Whitney   Built by the Whitney Sewing Machine Company, Paterson, New Jersey, from c1872 until c1880.

Whitney & Lyons   The product of the US patent of 1854 granted to T. E. Weed. The machine was built by Whitney &

Lyons from c1859 until c1865, when the company was renamed the Weed Sewing Machine Company and incorporated T. E. Weed's other manufacturing interests.

Wickersham   Built by the Butterfield & Stevens Manufacturing Company, Boston, Mass, from 1853. It is not known when production ceased.

Willcox & Gibbs   Chain-stitch machine built by the Willcox & Gibbs Sewing Machine Company, New York, from 1857. This was the partnership of James and Charles (the son) Willcox and James E. A. Gibbs. The machine employed the patents of Gibbs dated 1856 and 1857 (see Fig 6 and page 53). In 1867 the London offices were located at 135 Regent Street. Prices at that time in England ranged from £8 to £15. The company still exists in 1973.

Williams   No particulars known. Possibly made by C. W. Williams Manufacturing Company, Montreal, Ontario, Canada, or by the Williams & Orvis Sewing Machine Company, Boston, Mass.

Williams & Company, J. D., Manchester, England   One surviving example resembles Dietrich machines and it is likely that Williams were importers or agents of German-built machines.

Williams Manufacturing Company, C. W., Montreal, Ontario, Canada   Between c1880 and c1890 the company built the Helpmate and New Williams machines. There is a possibility that the Williams sewing machine was also made by this company.

Williams & Orvis   Built by the Williams & Orvis Sewing Machine Company, Boston, Mass, for a short period from c1859 until after 1860.

Willway, J. S., St Augustines Parade, Bristol, England   Agent for Willcox & Gibbs.

Wilson   Built by the W. G. Wilson Sewing Machine Company, Cleveland, Ohio, from about 1867. The company also produced the Buckeye, Improved Buckeye and New Buckeye machines from c1867 until c1876. The marque was still in existence in 1885.

A. B. Wilson Built by E. E. Lee & Company, New York, in 1851 and 1852 under Allen B. Wilson's 1850 patent. The company was a partnership of A. P. Kline and Edward Lee. See also Wheeler & Wilson.

A. B. Wilson's Patent Seaming Lathe See Wheeler & Wilson.

Windsor A single-thread machine built by the Vermont Arms Company, Windsor, Vermont, between 1856 and 1858. The company was succeeded by Lansom, Goodnow & Yale, makers of the Clark's Revolving Looper machine.

Winselmann Nahamaschine Built by Gustav Winselmann GmbH, Attenburg, Saxony. The company also made the Saxony and Titan machines. No production dates known.

Wonder (Probably the name of a shop) 4 Ludgate Street, London. In 1867 an advertisement under the name Wonder announced that the Judkins machine was marketed from this address.

Woolridge, Keene & Moore, Lynn, Mass   Makers of the Chamberlain machine for about a year, commencing in 1853.

CHRONOLOGY
OF THE SEWING MACHINE

Serial numbers of sewing machines quoted in this chronology must be regarded as approximate. Where given they indicate the highest number applied to a machine in that year. For instance, the date of a Singer New Family machine with the serial number 358,822, is 1869—above 283,044 (1868 highest number) and below 369,826 (1869). Two serial numbers were carried on Singer machines from 1857 until sometime in the 1880s. Grace R. Cooper in her book, *The Invention of the Sewing Machine*, says that until about 1873 there was a difference of exactly 4,000 in the two numbers (ie a machine would be marked 12,163 and directly below it would be marked 16,163).

'From 1873 the last three digits of the two numbers continued to be the same but the lower number might be much lower than either number used in earlier years. The larger number is believed to have been a record of total production while the lower number may have referred to a machine of a particular style. The Singer Company can shed no light on the meaning of the top (or lower of the two) serial numbers. Generally, in the earlier machines, the difference in the two numbers will not affect the dating of a machine by more than one year. Since dating by serial number can only be estimated, the two numbers do not add an appreciable variable prior to 1873. Only the larger number however, should be considered in dating machines after 1873.'

For example, 2,002,004–7,865,804 would indicate that it was built between 1886 and 1888.

American-built Singer sewing machines bearing serial numbers with prefix letters are thought to have been made in the twentieth century. For British-built Singers before 1900 there appears to be one high value number with no letter prefix. After 1900 British-built Singers were marked as follows:

M	1 to M	327,109	January 1900 to June 1900
P	1 to P	998,980	July 1900 to December 1901
R	1 to R	1,388,024	January 1902 to December 1903
J	1 to J	1,945,640	January 1904 to December 1905
S	1 to S	2,425,059	January 1906 to December 1907
V	1 to V	1,828,349	January 1908 to December 1909
F	1 to F	9,999,999	January 1910 to December 1920
Y	1 to Y	9,999,999	December 1920 to October 1935
EA	1 to EA	999,999	October 1935 to January 1937
EB	1 to EB	999,999	February 1937 to January 1939
EC	1 to EC	999,999	February 1939 to December 1940
ED	1 to ED	999,999	January 1941 to April 1947

Frister & Rossmann of Berlin is another manufacturer to use double serial numbers. Four examples of this make of machine in the author's collection are as follows: A treadle machine not showing an importer's name, so presumably built pre-c1898—251,538–82,538, a difference of 169,000; machine of Loewe importation (c1898–c1901)—3,604,078–628,078, a difference of 2,976,000; machine of Pierssene importation (c1901–14)—1,112,711; machine of Quitmann importation (post-1920)—64,428. It is difficult to deduce anything from these serial numbers, particularly the single numbers which seem to be diminishing rather than progressing.

The Willcox & Gibbs serial system is unreliable when dating European-sold machines. For instance, there exists a machine bearing the serial number 2552 which, if the regular system were used, places the manufacture in the year 1857, the first year of the company's production, whereas it is known that this machine was built much later, to be used, incidentally, in the hat trade in St Albans. Mr W. R. Pethin, Sales Director of Willcox & Gibbs's London office has given the following information: a machine built in 1879 had the serial number 369,947. For the period 1904–38:

1904	540,000	1912	580,000	1923	680,000
1906	550,000	1914	590,000	1930	690,000
1908	560,000	1916	650,000	1938	730,000
1911	570,000	1921	660,000		

This seems to indicate a very low production output and would appear to indicate UK sales only.

1755–1844 THE BACKGROUND STORY

1755 By the invention of an embroidery needle with a point at each end, Charles F. Weisenthal, a German mechanic living in London, could be said to have devised the eye-pointed needle, an indispensable feature in future sewing machines.

1790 17 July—Thomas Saint, a London cabinet maker, was granted British patent no 1,764, covering an 'Alternative New Method of Making and Completing Shoes'. The patent was filed with several other inventions by Saint and lay undiscovered until about 1873 (see entry for that year).

1793 Barthelemy Thimonnier, born at Arbresle, near Lyons, France.

1796 29 July—Walter Hunt, born at Martinsburg, New York. Hunt was the inventor of a workable sewing machine between the years 1832 and 1834.

1800 Balthasar Krems, a hosiery worker of Mayen, Germany, reported to have been using a stitching machine.

Thomas Saint, by now in Bristol, granted a British patent for improvements in steam engines.

1804 14 February—Thomas Stone and James Henderson—presumably British—granted a French patent covering a stitching machine involving the use of pincers to imitate the action of human fingers; not a commercial success.

1807 30 October—William and Edward Walter Chapman granted

British patent 3,078 covering a stitching machine to be used in the manufacture of belting from several strands of rope.

1810 Balthasar Krems (see above) produced a knitted peak cap stitched by a chain-stitch machine of his invention. No patent was issued and there are no records of any commercial use of the machine.

1811 27 October—Isaac Merritt Singer born at Pittstown, New York.

1813 Death of Balthasar Krems.

1814 Joseph Madersperger, a Viennese tailor, granted an Austrian patent for a stitching machine, presumably intended for embroidery: no commercial use was apparently made of the machine.

1818-19 About this time a sewing machine is thought to have been made at Monkton, Vermont. (The first report on the matter was published in 1867 naming one, John Knowles, as the inventor of the machine that is said to have used a single thread and a two-pointed needle. Later information names the Rev John Adam Dodge and a mechanic, John Knowles, as responsible for the machine, of which no material evidence exists.)

1819 9 July—Elias Howe Jr born at Spencer, Massachusetts.

1824 Allen Benjamin Wilson born at Willett, New York.

1826 10 March—Henry Lye granted US patent to cover a machine for stitching leather. No description has survived.

26 June—Walter Hunt granted US patent for his first invention— a machine for spinning hemp and flax.

1830 17 July—Barthelemy Thimonnier granted a French patent covering a sewing machine (see page 17).

1834 Between the years 1832 and 1834 in New York, Walter Hunt built a lock-stitch sewing machine. In 1834 Hunt sold some of his patent rights to George A. Arrowsmith of the Globe Stove Works, Gold Street, New York.

1838 Walter Hunt's daughter, Caroline, then aged fifteen, is said to have persuaded him to abandon the development of the sewing machine on the grounds that it would put seamstresses out of work.

1839 Joseph Madersperger in Austria was granted a patent for his second machine. Like the first design of 1814, this machine was not put to commercial use.

Isaac Merritt Singer sold his first invention—an excavator—for $2,000.

1841 4 May—British patent 8,948 granted to Edward Newton and Thomas Archbold for the machine designed for the embroidery of gloves; unlikely that it was put to commercial use.

Barthelemy Thimonnier had 80 sewing machines working in a Paris factory making army uniforms.

1842 21 February—US patent 2,466 granted to John J. Greenough for a running-stitch machine with an alternative back-stitch—the first recorded American patent specifically covering a sewing machine. From evidence it seems that only the patent model was built.

1843 4 March—Benjamin W. Bean granted US patent 2,982 for a running-stitch machine. Elements of this invention were later used by manufacturers in commercially available machines.

27 December—US patent 3,389 granted to George H. Corliss, a shopkeeper at Greenwich, New York, later to become an inventor and manufacturer of steam engines. The machine was intended for sewing leather boots and shoes.

1844 22 July—James Rodgers granted US patent 3,672 for a machine using principles resembling the B. W. Bean invention of the previous year.

October—Elias Howe Jr completed his first prototype sewing machine.

7 December—John Fisher and James Gibbons granted British patent 10,424 for a two-thread shuttle machine with several eye-pointed needles, the first recorded patent for a machine using this combination. It is unlikely that the machine was put to commercial use.

TEN GOLDEN YEARS OF INVENTION 1845–54

1845 Thimonnier, with outside financial assistance, started the world's first sewing machine factory at Villafranche-sur-Saône, France, and developed a machine to make 200 stitches per minute.

April—Elias Howe's machine was used to sew the seams for two men's suits (see page 18).

1846 10 September—Elias Howe granted US patent 4,750 covering his sewing machine.

1847 5 February—Elias and Amasa Howe set sail for England in an attempt to have the sewing machine accepted.

Allen Benjamin Wilson conceived the idea of a sewing machine.

1848 8 February—Barthelemy Thimonnier and associate Jean Marie Magnin granted British patent covering a sewing machine. Outbreak of the French Revolution brought Thimonnier's production in France to a halt.

28 November—John A. Bradshaw granted US patent 5,942 to cover improvements in the Howe patent of 1846.

1849 6 February—Charles Morey and Joseph B. Johnson granted US patent 6,099 covering the invention of a sewing machine. Before the patent had been issued production of the machine had been started by Safford & Williams, Boston, Massachusetts.

April—Elias Howe returned to New York from England to discover that sewing machines were being produced in the USA. Howe raised sufficient funds for a friend, Anson Burlingame, to redeem machine no 1 that had been left in pawn in London.

8 May—John Bachelder granted US patent 6,439 for a sewing machine. (The rights of this patent were sold to I. M. Singer and became one of the important patents listed by the Sewing Machine Combination in 1856.)

8 May—Jotham S. Conant was granted a US patent for a machine which featured a means of keeping cloth taut while being sewn, an invention which seems not to have been commercially exploited.

2 October—Sherburne C. Blodgett and John A. Lerow granted US patent 6,766 for what was described a Rotary Sewing Machine. The machine was produced either before or from that date by Orson C. Phelps, Boston and by Goddard, Rice & Company, Worcester, Massachusetts.

2 October—granting of the renewal of the patent issued to James Rodgers in 1844, although no commercial success seems to have resulted.

1850 September—Isaac Merritt Singer completed the first prototype of his sewing machine after seeing a Blodgett & Lerow machine at Orson Phelps's workshop a month earlier. He was joined in his venture by Phelps and by George Zieber, a Boston Publisher. The application for a US patent was made sometime between September 1850 and March 1851 but production was started as soon as the machine proved workable.

20 September—Barthelemy Thimonnier and Jean Marie Magnin were granted a US patent covering the Thimonnier machine that had received a British patent in 1848.

September—Sewing machines demonstrated at The Massachusetts Charitable Mechanics Association Exhibition, where a Blodgett & Lerow machine was awarded a Silver Medal, and one by A. B. Wilson won a Bronze Medal.

12 November—Allen Benjamin Wilson (see previous entry) was granted US patent 7,776. Forced through lack of funds to sell half his interest to A. P. Kline and Edward Lee who traded under the name E. E. Lee & Company, New York.

25 November—Wilson further pressed to sell the remaining share for $2,000, retaining only very limited rights.

Elias Howe brought law suits for infringement of patent against other manufacturers. Howe himself had, by now, a few machines working in New York factories.

Joseph Madersperger, the Viennese who had invented sewing machines in 1814 and 1839, died in disillusionment and poverty.

Abraham Bartholf started building sewing machines in New York, based on the Blodgett & Lerow patent of the previous year.

The American manufacturing company of Jones & Lee was founded.

1850 Serial Numbers:

Bartholf	20
Singer	100

1851 11 February—William O. Grover and William E. Baker, tailors of Boston, Mass, granted US patent 7,931. Grover & Baker Sewing Machine Company founded.

12 August—A. B. Wilson granted US patent for rotary hook mechanism. Prior to this date Wilson had severed his connection with Kline and Lee (E. E. Lee & Company) to join Nathaniel Wheeler to form the Wheeler, Wilson Company, Watertown, New York.

12 August—I. M. Singer granted US patent 8,294. The application had been filed on 16 April (see page 35).

Castle Gardens Exhibition, New York, where several sewing machines, including that of Elias Howe, were on display. Great Universal Exhibition, London, where Thimonnier's and another French machine, two US-built machines, including a Morey & Johnson, and one by British inventor, Charles Judkins (see Fig 4), were demonstrated. The makes of the other American and—this would greatly interest historians—the second French machine are not known.

1851   Serial Numbers:

Bartholf	50
Grover & Baker	500
Singer	900
Wheeler, Wilson	200

1852   15 June—A. B. Wilson granted US patent covering the stationary bobbin.

22 June—Grover & Baker granted US patent 9,053 for mechanism to form double-looped stitch.

Among the manufacturers to establish themselves in 1852 were the Avery Sewing Machine Company, New York; Bradbury & Company, Oldham, England; and Symon's Patent, London (information about the latter is taken from an advertisement that appeared in 1868).

1852 Serial Numbers:

Bartholf	100
Grover & Baker	1,000
Singer	1,711
Wheeler, Wilson	650

1853 29 March—Thomas C. Thompson granted US patent for a sewing machine mechanism, which was used on the productions of The American Magnetic Sewing Machine Company. About 40 of these machines were built between March and September.

May—Elias Howe granted a licence to Wheeler, Wilson & Company to enable them openly to make use of his patent. Licences to other manufacturers followed within a few months. For the prolonged law suits brought by Howe against manufacturers, Walter Hunt had been pursued by the defendants to build a replica of his 1834 machine.

William Frederick Thomas in London, who had purchased the rights to Howe's machine in 1847, was granted a British patent for a lock-stitch mechanism and commenced selling sewing machines under his name.

US patent was granted for Sweet's binder attachment. A. B. Wilson's health deteriorated and he was forced to retire from active participation in the Wheeler, Wilson company.

At The Industry of All Nations Exhibition in New York, a Watson single-looping machine was shown by Jones & Lee. They had previously displayed a two-thread lock-stitch Watson at the 1850 Massachusetts exhibition.

The Silver Medal award at the 1853 Massachusetts Charitable Mechanics Association Exhibition went to a machine designed by Nehemiah Hunt.

1853 Serial Numbers:

Bartholf	235
Grover & Baker	1,658
N. Hunt	100
Nichols & Bliss	28
Singer	2,521
Wheeler, Wilson	1,449

1854 The Singer company acquired the rights of the 1849 patent issued to Morey & Johnson and, in June, was granted the reissue of a patent covering a yielding pressure mechanism.

1 July—The verdict of the court being in favour of Howe in his

infringement suits, the Singer company was ordered to pay $15,000 to Howe.

Amasa Howe formed the Howe Sewing Machine Company, New York, and built machines under licence of his brother Elias.

19 December—A. B. Wilson granted US patent covering four-motion feed (see Fig 5).

1854 Serial Numbers:

Bartholf	290	N. Hunt	368
American Magnetic	600	J. B. Nichols & Co	245
A. B. Howe	60	Singer	3,400
Grover & Baker	3,893	Wheeler, Wilson	2,205

YEARS OF EXPANSION 1855–64

1855 22 May—T. J. W. Robertson granted US patent for a chain-stitch mechanism used by Robertson and D. W. Clark on several highly ornate machines such as the Cherub, Foliage and Dolphin designs.

James E. A. Gibbs decided to design a simpler sewing machine after seeing an illustration of a Grover & Baker machine.

1855 Serial Numbers:

Bartholf	321	Nichols, Leavitt & Co	397
Grover & Baker	5,038	Singer	4,283
A. B. Howe	113	Wheeler, Wilson	3,376
N. Hunt	442		

1856 27 May—Grover & Baker granted a US patent for fitted wooden cases (see page 53).

This was the year in which the Sewing Machine Combination was formed and in which the Singer company introduced instalment purchase—the pioneer of all hire-purchase schemes.

Among the new sewing machine companies to start production were Milton Finkle, Boston, Mass; C. R. Gardner, Detroit, Mich; Emery, Houghton & Company, Boston, Mass; L. W. Langdon,

Florence, Mass; and the Vermont Arms Company, Windsor, Vermont, turned their attention to sewing machines.

1856 Serial Numbers:

Bartholf	356	Hunt & Webster	622
Finkle	200	Nichols, Leavitt & Co	632
Grover & Baker	7,000	Singer	6,847
A. B. Howe	166	Wheeler & Wilson	5,586

1857 2 June—James E. A. Gibbs granted US patent 17,427 (see page 53). Willcox & Gibbs Sewing Machine Company was formed in New York, the machines selling for $50.

5 July—Barthelemy Thimonnier died at Amplepuis in poverty at the age of sixty-four.

26 August—S. B. Ellithorp granted a US patent for a two-thread, stationary bobbin mechanism which was intended for the highly decorative Squirrel machine (see Fig 23). Patent rights were sold under the name of Ellithorp & Fox but it is not certain if the machine was put into production. At the Massachusetts Charitable Mechanics Association Exhibition the Silver Medal was awarded to Hunt & Webster.

1857 Serial Numbers:

Bartholf	387	Leavitt & Co	827
Finkle	450	Singer	10,477
Grover & Baker	10,681	Wheeler & Wilson	10,177
A. B. Howe	299	Willcox & Gibbs	10,000
N. Hunt	1,075		

1858 5 January—David W. Clark granted US patent 19,015 in respect of a chain-stitch mechanism used on the ornamental Dolphin machine, the first of a number of patents issued to Clark in this year: 19,072 (12 Jan); 19,129 (19 Jan); 19,409 (23 Feb); 19,732 (23 March); 20,481 (8 June); and 21,322 (31 Aug).

9 March—Charles Raymond granted US patent 19,612 featuring a hinged pressure foot acting as a top feed, a conception which was

incorporated in the New England machines made by Nettleton & Raymond, Bristol, Conn.

6 April—A. Bartholf granted US patent 19,823 covering an improved shuttle carrier.

6 July—Lynan R. Blake granted US patent 20,775 covering a leather stitcher. This machine, using a hooked needle, was an important development in the boot and shoe industry.

5 October—Joseph Hendrick, granted US patent 21,722 covering the simple and inexpensive Sewing Shears (see page 71).

30 November—Albert H. Hook granted US patent 22,179 covering a simple mechanism involving a barbed needle (see Fig 19). Singer introduced the Family machine priced at $100.

1858 Serial Numbers:

Bartholf	590	Leavitt & Co	902
Finkle	700	Singer	14,071
Grover & Baker	15,752	Wheeler & Wilson	18,155
A. B. Howe	478	Willcox & Gibbs	20,000
N. Hunt	1,565		

1859 Singer introduced the Transverse Shuttle Machine Letter A priced at $75

Walter Hunt died.

In England the London office of Willcox & Gibbs was opened; Frederick W. Parker of Sheffield was granted a British patent for a looper that was used on the Weir sewing machine built from 1872. William Jones started making small steam engines at Audenshaw, Lancashire. He very soon commenced manufacture of sewing machines under licence of Howe, and A. B. Wilson.

1859 Serial Numbers:

Bartholf	1,337	Leavitt & Co	1,115
Finkle & Lyon	950	Singer	25,024
Grover & Baker	26,033	Wheeler & Wilson	39,461
A. B. Howe	1,399	Willcox & Gibbs	30,000
Ladd, Webster & Co	3,353		

1860 Elias Howe applied for and received a seven-year extension of his patent. His special royalty was reduced from $5 to $1 for each machine.

The Sewing Machine Combination licence was reduced from $15 to $7 per machine.

Willcox & Gibbs dropped hand-turned machines from the US market.

R. M. Wanzer opened a factory at Hamilton, Ontario, Canada, making the Time Utilizer machine.

At the Ninth Massachusetts Charitable Mechanics Association Exhibition in Boston, Silver Medals were awarded to the Boudoir and to Finkle & Lyon. A Bronze Medal was won by Greenman & True—who, at this exhibition, entered their machine under the name Morse & True.

1860 Serial Numbers:

Finkle & Lyon	1,500	Singer	43,000
Florence	500	Wheeler & Wilson	64,563
Grover & Baker	44,869	Willcox & Gibbs	40,000
Leavitt & Co	1,436		

1861 The American Civil War began. Although sewing machine manufacture continued, the war reduced the number of machines being made, many companies turning their attention to war materials.

The Union Army placed orders for machine-stitched bootees.

5 March—J. L. Hyde was granted US patent covering a glass pressure foot, a feature to be used on Wheeler & Wilson machines.

1861 Serial Numbers:

Finkle & Lyon	3,000	Singer	61,000
Florence	2,000	Wheeler & Wilson	83,119
Grover & Baker	63,705	Willcox & Gibbs	50,000
Leavitt & Co	1,757		

Probably some 3,000 Greenman & True machines had been built, and less than 1,000 Lester machines had been made since 1858, and before the close of 1861.

1862 At the International Exhibition in London a machine built by the Howe Sewing Machine Company (Amasa's factory) was given the highest award. Also at this exhibition a Grover & Baker machine was displayed by Newton Wilson, who, presumably, had not yet started production of machines under his own name.

13 May—Aaron Palmer granted US patent 35,252 covering a running-stitch mechanism on which the Fairy type machine built by several American manufacturers in the 1860s was based.

1862 Serial Numbers:

Finkle & Lyon	5,000	Singer	79,396
Florence	8,000	Wheeler & Wilson	111,321
Grover & Baker	82,641	Willcox & Gibbs	60,000
Leavitt & Co	2,077		

1863 Isaac Merritt Singer withdrew from active business life and the Singer concern was reorganised into the Singer Manufacturing Company.

21 April—US patent number 38,246 to Shaw & Clark, covering a running-stitch machine.

17 November—No 40,622 to W. D. Heyer for a pocket sewing machine.

Madam Demorest of New York, began to manufacture the Fairy sewing machine to Aaron Palmer's patent of 1862.

1863 Serial Numbers:

Finkle & Lyon	7,000	Singer	99,426
Florence	20,000	Wheeler & Wilson	141,099
Grover & Baker	101,477	Willcox & Gibbs	70,000
Leavitt & Co	2,400		

1864 The end of the American Civil War.

Machines made by the Willcox & Gibbs Sewing Machine Company were marked Willcox & Gibbs. Prior to this date machines were marked 'James Willcox, New York (or Philadelphia). J. E. A. Gibbs' Patent ——'.

William A. Mack & Company, of Norwalk, Ohio, established. The company exists to this day as the Domestic Sewing Machine Company, a subsidiary of the White Sewing Machine Company, Cleveland, Ohio.

1864 Serial Numbers:

Finkle & Lyon	9,000	Singer	123,058
Florence	35,000	Wheeler & Wilson	181,161
Grover & Baker	120,313	Willcox & Gibbs	80,000
Leavitt & Co	2,900		

FIRM FOUNDATIONS

1865 British patent granted to Bradbury & Company, Oldham, England.

In America the Singer Manufacturing Company introduced the New Family machine.

At the Tenth Massachusetts Charitable Mechanics Association Exhibition, Boston, the Silver Medals were awarded to Florence and Globe machines.

J. G. Folsom exhibited a New England machine with the Globe of his manufacture.

1865 Serial Numbers:

Finkle & Lyon	11,000	Singer	149,399
Florence	50,000	Wheeler & Wilson	220,318
Grover & Baker	139,148	Willcox & Gibbs	90,000
Leavitt S.M. Co	3,900		

1866 The foundation of the Goodspeed & Wyman company in America, which built the Bartlett machine until 1872 when production was undertaken by the Bartlett Sewing Machine Company, New York.

1866 Serial Numbers:

Bartlett	1,000	Leavitt S.M. Co	4,900
Finkle & Lyon	13,000	Singer	180,360
Florence	60,000	Wheeler & Wilson	270,450
Grover & Baker	157,886	Willcox & Gibbs	100,000

1867 The Howe patent expired despite an application for a further extension.

3 October—Elias Howe died. It was estimated he had received $2 million in royalties since 1856. Howe's own declared figure was $1,185,000.

The name of Finkle & Lyon sewing machines was changed to Victor.

In London, Wonder of Ludgate Street were marketing the Judkins sewing machine, and James Weir was selling the Lady's at £4.

William F. Thomas, who purchased the British patent rights of Elias Howe's machine, had premises in Cheapside and St Paul's Churchyard.

1867 Serial Numbers:

Bartlett	3,126	Leavitt S.M. Co	5,951
Bartram & Fanton	2,958	Singer	223,414
Finkle & Lyon	15,490	Wheeler & Wilson	308,505
Florence	70,534	Willcox & Gibbs	115,000
Grover & Baker	190,886		

1868 In London, Newton Wilson donated four sewing machines to the Science Museum. Symon's Patent, with premises in Blackfriars, were advertising the Gem at £4 and White (or Whight) & Mann were selling Alberta and Excelsior machines.

In the USA the General Favorite machines were introduced by the Weed Sewing Machine Company, Hartford, Conn.

1868 Serial Numbers:

Bartram & Fanton	3,958	Leavitt S.M. Co	6,951
Finkle & Lyon	17,490	Singer[1]	283,044
Florence	82,534	Wheeler & Wilson	357,856
Grover & Baker	225,886	Willcox & Gibbs	130,000
Howe Machine Co	46,000 (no figures available before this year)		

1869 British patent granted to William Jones who then commenced to manufacture his own invention. Prior to this he had built both Howe and A. B. Wilson machines under licence.

The Eleventh Massachusetts Charitable Mechanics Association

Exhibition was held in Boston where a Globe machine was again awarded a Silver Medal. A Bronze Medal went to a Bartram & Fanton.

The American Buttonhole, Overseaming and Sewing Machine Company was founded at Bridgeport, Conn, producing 7,792 machines in the first year.

Other 1869 Serial Numbers:

Bartram & Fanton	4,958	Leavitt S.M. Co	7,722
Finkle & Lyon	18,830	Singer	369,826
Florence	96,195	Wheeler & Wilson	436,722
Grover & Baker	261,004	Willcox & Gibbs	145,000
Howe Machine Co	91,843		

1870 A directory published in this year listed 69 sewing machine manufacturers in the United States.

Shanks's improved bobbin winder was granted a US patent. In England the patent was issued under which the Maxfield machine was built in Birmingham.

William Jones opened a new sewing machine factory at Guide Bridge, Lancashire.

1870 Serial Numbers:

American Buttonhole, Overseaming & S.M.	22,366	A. B. Howe (in 1870) (no figs available for 1860–70)	20,051
Bartram & Fanton	5,958	Howe Machine Co	167,000
Finkle & Lyon	21,250	Singer	497,660
Florence	113,855	Wheeler & Wilson	519,930
Grover & Baker	338,407	Willcox & Gibbs	160,000

1871 It is reported that some 700,000 sewing machines were built in the United States in this year.

G. Beckwith was granted a US patent covering a simple machine operated like a pair of scissors.

Willcox & Gibbs were granted a US patent for the clip-on spool holder.

Attachment patents in the United States during this year included Kerr's Needle Threader, Spoul's Braid Guide and, indicative of things to come, Jones's Electro-motor.

In England Harris & Judson were granted a patent on which the Challenge machine was built by the Imperial Sewing Machine Company, Birmingham.

1871 Serial Numbers:

American Buttonhole, Overseaming & S.M.	42,488	Grover & Baker	389,246
		Howe Machine Co	301,010
Bartram & Fanton	6,962		
Beckwith	3,500	Singer	678,921
Finkle & Lyon	28,890	Wheeler & Wilson	648,456
Florence	129,802	Willcox & Gibbs	190,127

1872 23 February—James Weir, London, granted a British patent for 'Improvements in Sewing machines and sewing machine needles', and production of the Weir machine was commenced. Husqvana in Sweden began the production of sewing machines. Harris's Thread Cutter patented in the USA.

1872 Serial Numbers:

American Buttonhole, Overseaming & S.M.	61,419	Grover & Baker	441,257
		Howe Machine Co	446,010
Bartram & Fanton	7,961	Singer	898,680
Beckwith	7,500	Wheeler & Wilson	822,545
Finkle & Lyon	40,790	Willcox & Gibbs	223,766
Florence	145,592		

1873 Newton Wilson discovered Thomas Saint's 1790 patent for a sewing machine while researching at the London Patent Office where it had been lying since filed among several other applications made at the same time (see Fig 2 and page 17).
James Weir was granted his second sewing machine patent.
In America the Stockwell Brothers—sons-in-law of Elias Howe—purchased the Howe Sewing Machine Company which had been founded by Elias's brother Amasa.

1873 Serial Numbers:

American Buttonhole, Overseaming & S.M.	75,602	Grover & Baker	477,437
		Howe Machine Co	536,010
Bartram & Fanton	8,961	Singer	1,121,125
Beckwith	12,500	Wheeler & Wilson	941,735
Finkle & Lyon	48,240	Willcox & Gibbs	239,647
Florence	154,555		

In 1873 the Remington company began production of typewriters in their sewing machine factory.

1874 Newton Wilson built a replica of the 1790 Thomas Saint machine, but had to make modifications in order for it to work.

In the United States, A. B. Wilson was refused an extension of his patent. West's Thread Cutter was granted a US patent.

1874 Serial Numbers:

American Buttonhole,		Grover & Baker	497,438
Overseaming & S.M.	89,132	Howe Machine Co	571,010
Bartram & Fanton	9,211	Singer	1,362,805
Beckwith	18,000	Wheeler & Wilson	1,034,563
Finkle & Lyon	53,530	Willcox & Gibbs	253,357
Florence	160,072		

1875 23 July—The end of an era. Isaac Merritt Singer died at Torquay, England.

In the United States the pioneer company of Grover & Baker ceased production in this name and were succeeded by The Union Special Machine Company.

James Weir's third British patent was granted.

1875 Serial Numbers:

American Buttonhole,		Grover & Baker	512,439
Overseaming & S.M.	103,539	Howe Machine Co	596,010
Beckwith	23,000	Singer	1,612,658
Finkle & Lyon	59,635	Wheeler & Wilson	1,318,303
Florence	164,964	Willcox & Gibbs	267,879

1876 The replica of the 1790 Thomas Saint machine, built by Newton Wilson, was exhibited at the Centennial Show, Philadelphia.

A. B. Wilson again refused an extension of his US patent.

Thomas H. White founded the White Sewing Machine Company, Cleveland, Ohio. Prior to this White was engaged in the design and manufacture of sewing machines for many years, including involvement in Brattleboro and New England machines.

1876 Serial Numbers:

American Buttonhole,		Howe Machine Co	705,304
Overseaming & S.M.	121,477	Singer	1,874,975
Finkle & Lyon	65,385	Wheeler & Wilson	1,247,300[2]
Florence	167,942	White	9,000

1877 The Sewing Machine Combination was dissolved as the patents in the combination's pool were expiring. The term of Bachelder's US patent ended.

1877 Serial Numbers:

Singer	2,000,000
White	27,000
Willcox & Gibbs	279,637

1878 The replica of the 1790 Thomas Saint machine, built by Newton Wilson, was exhibited at the Paris Exposition Universelle.

1878 Serial Numbers:

White Sewing Machine Co 45,000

1879 The Singer Manufacturing Company introduced the oscillating hook with circular shuttle.

1879 Serial Numbers:

Willcox & Gibbs 369,947
(according to London Office figures)

1880 A directory published in this year listed 124 sewing machine manufacturers in the USA.

In Canada, the C. W. Williams Manufacturing Company, Montreal, introduced the New Williams machine, later to become known as the Helpmate.

1880 Serial Numbers:

Singer 3,000,000

1881 In the USA the Weed Sewing Machine Company introduced the Hartford machine.

A US patent was granted for the Rose embroiderer.

1882 The *American Mechanical Directory* depicted 68 types of mechanical stitching. Harris's buttonhole attachment, and Garvie & Wood musical cover for a sewing machine, were granted US patents.

1882 Serial Numbers:

Singer	4,000,000

1883 The Singer Manufacturing Company introduced the Improved Family machine.

About this time Hermann Loog of London started the importation of Frister & Rossmann machines from Berlin.

1884 In Canada the Gardner Sewing Machine Company, Hamilton, Ontario, began manufacturing.

1884 Serial Numbers:

Singer	5,000,000

1885 S. A. Rosenthal of Berlin was granted a patent for a pocket sewing machine.

The French manufacturers of Hurtu ceased production of sewing machines to concentrate, it is reported, on motor engineering.

1886 The Moldacot Pocket Sewing Machine Company started manufacture in London of machines based on the Rosenthal patent of 1885.

1886 Serial Numbers:

Singer	6,000,000

1888 29 April—Allen B. Wilson died.

1888 Serial Numbers:

Singer	7,000,000

1889 An electric motor was fitted to a Singer machine.

1889 Serial Numbers:

Singer	8,000,000

1890 A directory published in this year listed 66 sewing machine manufacturers in the USA.

1890 Serial Numbers:

Singer	9,000,000

1891 Serial Numbers:

Singer	10,000,000

1893 The Advance Premier machine was marketed by J. Theobold & Company, Farringdon Road, London, priced at 15 shillings.

1894 Newton Wilson presented his replica of the 1790 Thomas Saint machine to the Science Museum, London.

1898 S. Loewe, Fore Street, London, started importation of the German-built Frister & Rossmann machines.

1901 The franchise for Frister & Rossmann sewing machines was passed from S. Loewe to W Pierssenne, with offices still in Fore Street, London.

1902 James E. A. Gibbs died.

1905 The Singer Manufacturing Company took over the Wheeler & Wilson Sewing Machine Company.

1907 The Jones Sewing Machine Company, Guide Bridge, Lancashire, discontinued production of their bent back design.

1919 The son of William F. Thomas presented the Howe sewing machine, purchased by his father in the late 1840s, to the Science Museum, London.

1920 Importation into England of Frister & Rossmann machines undertaken by O. Quitmann, London.

1924 The White Sewing Machine Company, Cleveland, Ohio, acquired the Domestic Sewing Machine Company.

1925 Manufacture of Frister & Rossmann sewing machines taken over by Gritzer-Kayser. O. Quitmann continued the London agency.

For notes to this section see pages 162-3.

APPENDIX:
WHERE TO SEE
SEWING MACHINE COLLECTIONS

The world's finest assemblage of sewing machines is housed at the Museum of History and Technology, the Smithsonian Institution, Washington, DC, established in 1846 for the promotion and encouragement of original scientific research. Most of the historically important US patent models have been preserved there.

Until 1880 it was compulsory for a working model to accompany a patent application in the US. Were the nineteenth-century commissioners of the US Patent Office aware of the wealth of historical evidence they were accumulating when it was stipulated that a model had to be deposited? It is to be regretted that the requirements were not continued and that the practice was not observed elsewhere.

The majority of the early sewing machines in the Smithsonian collection were acquired in 1926 when the Patent Office disposed of hundreds of these models. Sometimes the models were built to the inventors' instructions by professional model makers such as James Willcox (see page 53). Most inventors however, through financial necessity, made their own.

In addition to the pre-production patent models, the Smithsonian houses a great many series-manufactured machines to which minor alterations have been made by inventors when applying for patents covering improvements of changes of design. Often these are the only examples of production models known to survive.

Among the collection of more than 700 sewing machine patent

models in the Smithsonian collection can be found John J. Greenough's running-stitch model of 1842, for which he was granted US patent 2,466—the first American patent to apply specifically to a sewing machine; Benjamin Bean's 1843 model (US patent 2,982); George Corliss's model, also of 1843, and numbers 1 and 2 models of Elias Howe. There are also John Bachelder's endless belt feed model of 1849, and Allen B. Wilson's patent models, the double-pointed shuttle machine of 1850 and the stationary bobbin model of 1852, but an example of his four-motion feed patent model is not known to exist.

Grover & Baker's two-thread double chain-stitch model of 1851 is in the Smithsonian collection, but one can look in vain for Isaac M. Singer's pre-production model. The first Singer in the collection is a production model, serial number 28. We have already mentioned the mystery about Singer's original patent application, which was never granted for some reason or other (see page 35). There must have been a model to accompany the original application. It could have been returned to the inventor if he abandoned the application. Why then did he not submit the model with his second application?

It is more likely that the original model was left at the Patent Office with the abandoned application. Some 76,000 patent models were ruined in a fire at the Patent Office in 1877, and over 3,000 abandoned models were sold at auction in 1908.[1] If the machine was disposed of in this way it is possible that it still survives.

The Science Museum in South Kensington, London, has a smaller but none the less important collection of sewing machines on public display. The star exhibit, of course, is the replica of the Thomas Saint machine of 1790, built by Newton Wilson in 1874. *Replica* is hardly the correct word because, although based on Saint's drawings and specification, Wilson had to make a number of modifications to the design in order to make it work. This does not mean that Saint did not build a working machine—he may have submitted his patent application before finding out by experiment that the conception was imperfect. However, it is generally thought that Saint did not actually construct his machine.

The Science Museum's copy of a Thimonnier machine is said to be 'of an early machine made in accordance with his patent. His later machines were different in some respects and did not have a fly wheel'.[2] This seems to contradict the evidence of an engraving of Thimonnier sitting at his machine in 1830 which was published in the *Sewing Machine News* of 1880. The machine shown in this engraving also does not have a fly wheel.

By 1845 Barthelemy Thimoniner had developed his invention to the extent that it would perform 200 stitches per minute. Six years later, the English inventor, Charles Judkins, exhibited a machine at the Great Exhibition that would make 500 stitches per minute. The Science Museum has a copy of the lock-stitch machine which, like all machines of the period, was intended for industrial use.

The Elias Howe model in the Science Museum is the third machine built by the pioneer. This one was for William Frederick Thomas after Howe's arrival in England in 1847. Although generally resembling the number 2 machine, now in the Smithsonian Institution in Washington, there are a few minor but interesting differences. Number 3 machine was donated to the Science Museum by Thomas's son in 1919. W. Thomas's own machine, for which he received a British patent in 1853, is exhibited at the Science Museum too. As far as can be ascertained, this is the only existing example of this particular machine.

The Science Museum's early Singer Perpendicular Action Sewing Machine differs from the 1851 (serial number 28) model in the Smithsonian in some details. Whereas the London machine carries the spool of thread on the back of the machine, the Smithsonian example has this over the needle on the sewing head, and closely resembles an illustration of 1853 in the American magazine *Illustrated News*.

The display at the Science Museum shows the development of mechanical sewing up to the present day. There are production models from Wheeler & Wilson, Grover & Baker, Willcox & Gibbs, James Weir, Singer, Jones, Howe, Moldacot and Husqvana.

Most municipal museums have sewing machines in their collections, mainly donated by local residents. Unfortunately, almost all museums suffer from shortage of display space and sewing machines, unless exceptional, are not considered worthy of taking space away from pieces of Roman pottery or stuffed wild life. Consequently, the machines are often relegated to storage cellars.

Yet a sewing machine collector should always keep contact with the curator of a local museum. Items are frequently offered which cannot be accepted because of restrictions of space, or because they are not considered to be of sufficient general historical importance. In such cases the curator welcomes having the name of a local specialist collector which can be passed on to whoever is willing to donate the machine.

For notes to this section see page 163

ʟ

NOTES

Chapter 2

1   Most authorities now believe this year to be 1873.
2   Obviously Saint was not influenced by Weisenthal's needle with an eye at the same end as the point.
3   The features of Howe's machine were that it had a grooved and curved eye-pointed needle carried on a vibrating arm. The loops of thread from the needle were locked by a shuttle-carried thread. The cloth was suspended vertically by pins on a baster plate—the length of each stitching operation depending upon the length of this plate, the cloth having to be removed and re-set before progressing with the stitching.
4   Elias Howe's machines no 1 and no 2 are now in the sewing machine collection of the Smithsonian Institution, Washington, DC. No 3 is in the Science Museum, London, donated by William Thomas's son in 1919. No 4 has not been located.

Chapter 3

1   Some sources give this number as 300.
2   *Great Britain: Her Finance & Commerce*, published by The Morning Post.
3   James Starley should not be confused with J. K. Starley, his nephew, also a cycle maker who, in 1877, was in partnership with W. Sutton in the Rover Cycle Company, which later turned its attention to making motorcycles and cars.

Chronology of the Sewing Machine

1   Advertising claims state that 59,629 Singer machines were sold in Britain in 1868.
2   Wheeler & Wilson introduced the No 8 in this year and a new numbering series was started.

Appendix

1   *The Invention of the Sewing Machine*, Grace R. Cooper (1968).
2   *Sewing Machines*, K. R. Gilbert (1970).

BIBLIOGRAPHY

Bartleet, H. W. *Bartleet's Bicycle Book* (1931)
Bernal, J. D. *Science and Industry in the Nineteenth Century* (1953)
Cooper, Grace Rogers. *The Invention of the Sewing Machine* (1968)
Ewers, William Baylor. *Sincere's History of the Sewing Machine* (1970)
Gilbert, K. R. *Sewing Machines* (1970)
Larsen, E. *Ideas and Inventions* (1960)
Lewton, Frederick L. *Servant in the House* (1929)
Moncrieff, D. Scott. *Victorian and Edwardian Motor Cars* (1955)
Pearsall, Ronald. *Collecting Mechanical Antiques* (1973)
Routledge, R. *Discoveries and Inventions of the Nineteenth Century* (1900)
Stambaugh, John P. *A History of the Sewing Machine* (1872)
also
Kelly's Directories and other commercial directories of industrial towns; the following periodicals are also useful: *Bygone & Veteran*; *Journal of Domestic Appliances and Sewing Machine Gazette*; *Sewing Machine News*; *Scientific American*.

ACKNOWLEDGEMENTS

The author would like gratefully to acknowledge the co-operation of many friends and correspondents with whom, over the years, he has had the pleasure of exchanging information. Special thanks are due to:

Mr J. N. Allen, BA, FLA, Brighton Public Libraries; Mr W. Best Harris, FL, Plymouth City Library; The Birmingham City Libraries; Mr Charles W. Black, MA, FLA, The Mitchell Library, Glasgow; Mr J. W. Carter, FLA, The Central Library, Cheltenham; Mr R. L. Casey, Dublin City Library; The Durham City Branch of the Durham County Library; Mrs Grace Rogers Cooper, The Smithsonian Institution; Mr P. R. Gifford, ALA, Colchester Borough Library; Mr K. R. Gilbert, MA, DIC, The Science Museum, London; Mr P. G. Gill, The Central Library, Northampton; Mr K. C. Harrison, MBE, FLA, Marylebone Library; Mr D. E. Hutchinson, Western Australia Museum; Mr A. G. Mitchell, City of Coventry Museum; The Oldham Public Reference Library; Mr D. F. Parker, FLA, Cheltenham Borough Library; Mr D. Taylor, The Central Library, Manchester; Mr Fred Taylor, FLA, Keighley Central Library. To Mrs Venia Ellis, The Singer Sewing Machine Company; Mr W. R. Pethin, Willcox & Gibbs Limited; Mr Derick Quitmann, Frister & Rossmann Sewing Machines; The Jones Sewing Machine Company Limited. To Mrs Elizabeth Chambers; Mrs V. Edenden; Mrs A. D. Macdonald; Mrs Vera Matthews; Mrs Imogen Nichols; Mrs M. Oliver; Mrs M. Rotter; Mrs I. E. Tutt. To Messrs Henry Cassen; S. J. Eade; J. Grant; Nicholas Hill; H. Roy Hudson; R. V. Langridge; Brian Matthews; F. A. Nicholls; T. F. Oliver; N. A. Parfitt; Peter Pollington; J. H. C. Proudfoot; David Sneller; C. W. Stace; Kenneth H. Swanson; A. Willmod, and thanks too to all the others who have given such great help at the many show events attended by the Veteran Machine Register.

INDEX

Figures in italic refer to illustrations

165

E41237

7.95

TJ510
J48   Jewell, Brian.
          Veteran sewing machines : a collector's guide / Brian Jewell.
       — 1st American ed. — South Brunswick : A. S. Barnes, 1975.
          172 p. : ill. ; 22 cm.

          Bibliography: p. 163.
          Includes index.
          ISBN 0-498-01714-1 : $7.95

          1. Sewing-machines—Collectors and collecting.   I. Title.

       TJ1510.J48   1975b   681'.7677   74-30539
                                                                  MARC

          Library of Congress   75